Praise for *How to R...*
by THE bOOK

"You don't have to be religious to appreciate the valuable lessons for life and business found in the Bible. In his new book, my friend, Dave Anderson, has captured some of the most meaningful examples of this ancient wisdom and combined it with his twenty-first century perspectives to help you find success in the marketplace and in life."

—*Jim Blasingame, small business expert, author, columnist, and host of The Small Business Advocate® Show*

"Dave Anderson has done a magnificent job of creating and presenting high-impact business strategies based upon biblical principles! Applying this blueprint will quickly elevate your personal leadership and transform your organization's results."

—*Doug Carter, Senior Vice President, EQUIP*

How *to* Run *Your* Business *by* THE BOOK

A Biblical Blueprint to
Bless Your Business
Revised and Expanded

DAVE ANDERSON

WILEY

John Wiley & Sons, Inc.

For general information on our other products and services or for technical support,
please contact our Customer Care Department within the United States at
(800) 762-2974, outside the United States at (317) 572-3993 or fax (317) 572-4002.

Wiley also publishes its books in a variety of electronic formats. Some content that
appears in print may not be available in electronic formats. For more information about
Wiley products, visit our web site at www.wiley.com.

ISBN 978-1-118-02237-5 (pbk); ISBN 978-1-118-09942-1 (ebk);
ISBN 978-1-118-09943-8 (ebk); ISBN 978-1-118-09944-5 (ebk)

Printed in the United States of America

10 9 8 7 6 5 4 3 2 1

This book is dedicated to the youth group at Noah's Ark Church in Ararat, Armenia. You are more than friends to me; you are an inspiration. You live your lives by THE BOOK. Let no one despise your youth!

Contents

Foreword

I've known Dave Anderson since 1998. I met him at the first Founder's Meeting in Atlanta for my nonprofit organization, EQUIP. EQUIP is committed to training and developing millions of godly leaders throughout the world in support of the Great Commission. Dave was attracted to EQUIP because of his passion for training, for leadership, and for making a difference in the lives of others. Over the years, I've come to appreciate Dave's communication skills, his commitment to biblical leadership principles, and his resounding business success. It is these three qualities that make him uniquely qualified to write *How to Run Your Business by THE BOOK*.

Dave has walked the walk as a leader who makes a difference. Although many authors have expertise in the arenas for which they write, fewer have actually experienced or accomplished substantial success with their expertise. Dave has both expertise and experience applying the strategies he presents in this book, and they have helped him create a solid track record of accomplishments from which you will learn and benefit. For three years he taught biblical leadership principles in Moscow for EQUIP, and he continues to invest time doing the same with leaders from Iran and Armenia. His company, LearnToLead, grows steadily each year despite challenging economic times and fierce competition because he has built it upon a foundation of biblical principles that he shares in each chapter of this book.

Over the years, I've noticed how Dave has increasingly woven biblical principles into his books and seminars. He's done this naturally, effectively, and without becoming preachy. I believe you'll appreciate his unique blend of business and the Bible as you discover dozens of timeless principles that will bring solutions and results to your organization. The techniques are effective because they are based on God's infallible word and promises. They will validate many of the things you've done in the past and bring attention to areas in which you need to make changes to become more successful. His instruction will challenge you, stretch you, and encourage you. As you incorporate the recommended changes into your personal leadership style and within your organization, you will realize results that are more significant and sustainable.

As a businessperson, you will appreciate that this work is written by a peer and not by an academic. Christians will especially value the principles in *How to Run Your Business by THE BOOK*. These principles will reinforce what they have intuitively known to be true but may have been reluctant to incorporate into a business arena where the pervasive "nice guys finish last" and "dog eat dog" mindsets are greatly at odds with how they believe they should conduct themselves in the workplace.

I cannot think of a more "real-world" approach for a business book than to combine the timeless wisdom of God with the actual successes of one who has applied those principles and now wants to share them with others. Incidentally, the ideas in *How to Run Your Business by THE BOOK* are just as applicable to the leaders of nonprofit organizations as they are to the heads of families. You will be able to apply what you learn to your personal life, community, and church. In fact, Chapter 3's "How to Overcome the Number One Cause of Management Failure" should be required reading for teachers, parents, spouses, and elected officials.

Your goal should not be to get through *How to Run Your Business by THE BOOK*. Rather, it should be to get *from* it. I encourage you to quickly apply what you learn because biblically based leadership principles have the potential to dramatically transform your business and your life. There is no time to waste. The world is crying out for biblically based leadership in all sectors of society—for leaders like you to shine a brighter light of character, competence, and compassion into your workplace, community, and family.

—Dr. John C. Maxwell
www.johnmaxwell.com

Preface

How to Run Your Business by THE BOOK is written for everyone wanting to build their organization or return it to a rock-solid foundation of Biblical principles. A biblically based foundation sustains success and transcends fads, trends, and best practices that are in vogue one year and out the next. When uncertainty reigns, it is natural to feel a sense of emptiness and disillusionment with the direction of business and the world, and start looking for something more reliable, tested, and tried. The best-selling book of all time, the Bible, answers the call. Although it is common to read the Bible for spiritual truths, I have found that many business leaders don't realize the vast wealth of wisdom available throughout its pages that would help them to hire and train the right people; hold them accountable; create vision, values, and performance expectations for their organization; elevate their own character and people skills; and manage their money. *How to Run Your Business by THE BOOK* tackles these issues and more, and provide proven strategies that you can begin to use immediately.

The Bible can make many people feel lost. They want to read and understand it but they don't know where to start. They become intimidated by its length and confused by its verbiage. My goal in this book is to take principles that might take you years or decades to discover on your own and put them in a workable, hands-on, easy-to-apply business format that you will internalize and implement with confidence and certainty. Although the Bible offers thousands more lessons to learn than what you will find in this book, what I've presented should suffice to dramatically change the results in any organization when applied as prescribed. You'll also be relieved to know that this book neither promotes nor disparages any particular denomination, but instead, it presents the facts for you to evaluate and interpret using your own good sense.

In most households, the Bible is like an exercise bike. It sits in a corner and doesn't get a whole lot of use. On special occasions, such as after making a New Year's Resolution, someone will crank the old relic up again, but on most days it's left alone and amounts to little more than décor. Even "religious" people who have attended church for decades remain woefully ignorant of what is in the Bible—except for maybe the Christmas or Easter stories—and can recite three Scriptures at the most (John 3:16 and "Jesus wept" being two of them!). If this describes you, you'll be relieved to hear that you don't have to know the Bible to benefit from, understand, or appreciate the strategies in each chapter. However, I believe that the more you read about THE BOOK, the more you will want to learn about it. This is what happened to me many years ago, and one of my greatest joys each day is spending one to two hours each morning studying the Bible, regardless of the day or where I happen to be in the world.

Here's a quick rundown of what you can expect to find in each chapter:

CHAPTER 1: A SIX-PACK OF PRINCIPLES FROM A KING AND THE KING

I present six dynamic principles based on the lives of David and Jesus that you can internalize into your own personal leadership style, to immediately and measurably elevate your effectiveness and results.

Chapter 2: Four Mandates to Maximize Your Time

Because most leaders work long and hard but fall a bit short on the "working smart" part of the equation, you'll learn four time management techniques they probably didn't teach you at the last business seminar you attended. They are unconventional yet highly effective.

Chapter 3: How to Overcome the Number One Cause of Management Failure

Please pay particular attention to this chapter because it has the most potential of all eight chapters to significantly impact your life at both work and at home. Chapter 3 helps you learn to deal with and overcome your ego and your pride, and it shows how every other conceivable management failure is rooted in the evils of ego.

Chapter 4: Five Steps to Build a Rock Solid Character

This isn't your typical chapter on character. I present a handful of character flaws in Chapter 4 that you may have given little thought or notice to in the past. However, following the steps to overcome these flaws will build for you a credibility and competence that will ensure you become a leader who lasts over the long haul, not another one of the many talented people we see in life who self-destruct by making poor character choices.

Chapter 5: The "High Five" Principles to Elevate Your People Skills

The "High Five" principles I present in Chapter 5 will help you to instantly impact others with stronger connections and build a higher level of personal charisma that you may not have thought possible.

CHAPTER 6: FOUR KEYS TO CREATE LIFE-WORK BALANCE

This section is the most popular chapter in my live workshops for business people, so I had to put it in this book. It will show you four key areas in which you must pursue life-work balance and provide strategies for addressing each area. This is the chapter you are most likely to reread and refer to again to improve your personal life as well as your effectiveness at work.

CHAPTER 7: HOW TO MANAGE YOUR MONEY BY THE BOOK

Look out! This chapter will challenge you perhaps more than any of the others. This is especially true with the strategies it presents for giving your money away, for not going into debt (yes, that means for your business too), and for making business partnerships. Keep an open mind because THE BOOK's principles for money will take you farther, and faster than you could ever expect, from "becoming wise in your own eyes" concerning money.

CHAPTER 8: FOUR STEPS TO BUILD YOUR TEAM BY THE BOOK

Many books fizzle out by the final chapters, so I made a special effort to finish strong with what I believe you will agree is one of the strongest chapters in the book. It offers real-world strategies for hiring, creating vision, establishing values, setting performance expectations, holding others accountable, and building an inner circle of leaders to help accelerate the growth of your organization.

CHAPTER 9: HOW TO LEAD THROUGH CRISIS

This essential chapter is new to this revised and expanded edition of *How to Run Your Business by THE BOOK*. Every leader will be faced with crises in their work and personal lives. This chapter will arm you with the specific and unique strategies required to continue to get results as you face a crisis. It includes four common temptations leaders fall prey to during a crisis that you must be aware of and overcome.

APPENDIX: QUICK SCRIPTURAL REFERENCE GUIDE BY THE BOOK

Don't even think about skipping the Appendix! I've given you 42 commonly asked business questions with corresponding scriptural references that provide answers. Consider the Appendix as "God's Playbook" for running your business day in and day out.

VALUE-ADDED CHAPTER FEATURES

Each chapter opens with *Genesis*, which lays the foundation and creates perspective for the chapter's content.

Throughout the book are *By THE BOOK Blessings*. These are a combination of concise Scriptures and business wisdom sound bites, interspersed throughout the chapters to add color and depth to the topics presented.

You will also find an array of *By THE BOOK Lessons in Leadership* scattered throughout the pages that relate actual biblical stories and analogies in support of the prescribed strategies.

Prior to each chapter summary, I've included a brief *Shine the Light* essay; these are unique to this revised and expanded edition of *How to Run Your Business by THE BOOK*. These deeper insights are based on the principle found in Psalms 19:8 (*"The commandment of the Lord is pure, enlightening the eyes"*) and Psalms 119:130 (*"The entrance of Your words gives light; it gives understanding to the simple."*) Thus, *Shine the Light* is designed to help you go from merely knowing to truly understanding the strategies provided in each chapter, and how you can apply them to your life.

Each chapter concludes with a brief summary of key points and *Revelation*: final thoughts on the content that help you to understand and apply what you read.

To help you reflect on the points covered and consider how to apply them in your organization, there are a handful of *Action Exercise* questions that complete each chapter. By taking just a few moments to work through these questions, you will exponentially increase your retention and elevate the likelihood that you will follow through and convert knowledge into action that brings results.

Throughout *How to Run Your Business by THE BOOK*, there are recurring principles that cover accountability, building a team, the dangers of pride, and more. Just as themes recur throughout the Bible to highlight their importance, the same holds true in this book. Pay particular attention to recurring themes because they have the potential to quickly transform your leadership style and organization.

Keep a Bible and highlighter handy as you read each chapter, and don't be in a hurry to move on to what is next until you fully understand and have considered how to apply what you've already learned. The Bible was designed for a lifetime of study and application. Because this book is based on biblical principles, going slow and deep will benefit you more than racing quickly across the surface.

My hope for you as you read and apply the principles in *How to Run Your Business by THE BOOK* is found in Isaiah 58:11:

> The Lord will guide you continually, and satisfy your soul in drought, and strengthen your bones; you shall be like a watered garden, and like a spring of water whose waters do not fail.

Acknowledgments

I would like to express immense gratitude to my wife, Rhonda, for her unwavering support as I wrote this book. I also want to credit her with giving me the idea and encouragement to write the *How to Run Your Business by THE BOOK* workshop, which was the basis for this book.

Thanks also to Bill Gothard and his team at the Institute for Basic Life Principles. Their *Daily Success Scripture Meditation* program and *Financial Freedom* series have had a significant impact on my writing and on my life. I would like to also express gratitude to Larry Richards and his insightful Bible commentary I enjoy each day as part of the *Living Christian* software program. Larry, your wisdom has made reading the Bible fun and adventuresome!

To Matt Holt and Dan Ambrosio at John Wiley & Sons: Your encouragement and responsiveness to the concept of *How to Run Your Business by THE BOOK* has been awesome! This is my tenth book with you guys, and you're the best. You let your writers write, and you do what you say you'll do. An author can ask for nothing more.

To our thousands of customers at LearnToLead, thank you for your support, your friendship, and your feedback over these many years. You are a gift to me.

John Maxwell, you have influenced me in more ways than you can imagine or than I can count. Thank you for your heart, your expertise, and for EQUIP. Some of the most meaningful times in my life have been teaching your courses to hungry-for-knowledge leaders in Russia, Armenia, and from Iran.

To my Christian brothers and sisters in Russia, Armenia, and Iran whom I have had the pleasure to teach, befriend, and love, thank you for your prayers for this book and for me and my family as I have written it. I will be with you again soon.

Lord, I have thanked You many times for this chance to tell the world more about You and Your BOOK in this book, but I want to make it official and in print! Of all people I don't know why You chose me for this, but I am humbled and grateful that You did. My sincere prayer is that I did not let You down.

Introduction

Why do authors write books? In most cases, it's not for the money. In fact, most of the authors I know write books to help others make a difference in their lives. If the book is successful and leads to financial rewards, that's great; however, for most of us, making a difference is more important than making money.

I had written nine books prior to publishing *How to Run Your Business by THE BOOK: A Biblical Blueprint to Bless Your Business*. Over the years, I have been blessed by hundreds of kind e-mails and letters explaining to me the impact of the books I wrote on the lives and careers of readers. But no other work brought the volume and intensity of testimonies from readers as did *How to Run Your Business by THE BOOK*. The acclaim had nothing to do with my writing style or creativity. Rather, it was because the book was based on life-changing biblical principles that supersede the best of man's wisdom and best practices. In letter after letter, I witnessed the unmistakable potential God's power still has to change lives and businesses when people apply His principles. Take a look:

> Hi Dave,
> Management Consultant Michael Costantini and I have read dozens upon dozens of self improvement type

books. We both recently "actively" read *How to Run Your Business by THE BOOK*. We both read it slowly and purposefully, underscoring passages and writing notes in the margins. We don't typically read books for the sake of reading them. Instead, we read books and put the best ideas, principles, skills, and character traits into action. We think of our business as our Dojo for honing our disciplines and the disciplines of our employees. Mike is very active in his small groups and church community. He was so impressed, he felt compelled to send out an e-mail to 100+ family, friends, and associates telling them about your book and including a link to your YouTube videos.

Our business, Equilibrium, was founded on the idea of finding "balance" in multiple areas—health, spiritual, family & friends, career, continuing education, personal finance, community service to others, and hobbies. People living in balance are happy people. Happy people are much more productive. We feel fortunate that our business (Equilibrium) is already doing many of the principles you articulated; however, *we found many new gems that we will incorporate into our business practices*. In January, Mike and I are actively revamping our "Professional Development Program." We are excited to incorporate much of what we have recently learned from reading your book, and we feel really good that the principles stem from THE BOOK.

Perhaps someday we will meet face-to-face.

Thank you. God bless!

—Glen Hampton
President
Equilibrium IT Solutions, Inc.

Dear Dave,

I'd like to personally thank you for responding to God's call by writing *How to Run Your Business by THE BOOK*! I have been in the wake of a spiritual and professional sea of mediocrity, and God chose your book (and His by way of yours) to speak directly to me. I'm sure you're over-whelmed with e-mails, but I'd like to explain:

I'm a 36-year-old software sales professional who was promoted in January of 2008 to run a team and carry a $13M quota. After two years, I was demoted due to poor performance. Like you, I made many mistakes as a new and young manager, and unfortunately, my mistakes temporarily cost me a career progression that mapped to my "Divine calling." Your book is inspiring to me, as I've felt for my entire professional career that I've been called to run a business and then write a book on how to implement "Christ-centered" leadership tactics to the secular work environment. My calling was revealed in grad school when I wrote a paper on instituting bibli-cally centered ethics in corporate America.

So many of your principles are ones that I have tried to deploy, but there were many "a-ha" moments that were revealed through you by our gracious Father. I won't detail all of them, but here are a few:

— *Pride is "my sin of choice" and 100% was the culprit to my core and failure . . . not happenstance, bad timing, or inability to execute on team changes that could have turned my territory around.*
— *Positioning, spinning, and the tweaking of a message is nothing short of . . . a lie. Anything else but truth will ruin my reputation!*
— *Our Savior was a time management czar . . . never analyzing His strategies of how He spent time with His own team . . . I spent too much time with the bottom attempting to normalize them!*

The single largest "a-ha" moment in this book was this: I now have a manual to which I can combine my passion for business *and* most importantly utilize for my daily quiet time (thank you for tethering scripture throughout your book). I became a Christian at 9, and like many mature Christians, have seen ups and downs over time in my spiritual walk. Over the past few years, I've been in a state of spiritual mediocrity, self-reliance, and self-focus . . . and have been awaiting and fearing a Divine shaking. As I sat on the plane while reading your book, it was clear . . . My God ran to me and chose not to chastise me, but love me!

Father, bless my brother Dave for following Your guidance and nudging when writing this book. He chose to use Your words, not his, which in turn will make this book perfect. Protect Dave and his family from the attacks of Satan and his army, and I beg that You would utilize the success of his book as a platform to glorify Jesus Christ.

Your Brother in Christ and "Hundred-Fold Reader,"
— Name withheld

Now tell me, how can you put a price on knowing that you were allowed to play the role of messenger to communicate God's truths to these readers and help them change their outlooks and life?

Here's another letter that demonstrates how the principles in *How to Run Your Business by THE BOOK* relate to both one's personal life and career.

Hi Dave,
I hate you. Okay, just kidding. For the second time, I'm reading the chapter in the book on pride. I am the CEO of two organizations, and I have my own marketing business also. Where your book gently (and not so gently) stuck the knife in my heart, twisted it, and left me bleeding, was in my marriage of 24 years.

I've been praying to God for insight into my part in what has become quite a boring, unromantic relationship. I am the source of our conflict (Oh, did I really write that?). Yep. Thank you for letting God use you to convict me.

—Name withheld

Like any book, sermon, or seminar, the strategies in *How to Run Your Business by THE BOOK* will only help you if you apply them. Simply knowing what to do is never enough, because life rewards action, not knowledge. Jesus made this clear in John 13:17 when He said: *"If you know these things, blessed are you if you do them."* Thus, as you read each chapter and consider the points that will help you elevate your business and life, you're wise to remember that if nothing changes, then nothing changes. You'll need to take the first step, because you cannot attain greater levels of success by remaining passive and waiting for the things around you to change. Rather, you must change what's within you— your heart and mind—so that you can then change what's around you.

In the seventeenth chapter of Acts, opponents of Christianity—when complaining to their rulers about Christians who had come to their city—exclaimed, *"These who have turned the world upside down have come here too"* (Acts 17:6). The men and women being spoken of in this passage didn't turn the world upside down by defending or nurturing the status quo. Instead, they took action based on God's principles, leveraging Christ's light to dispel darkness in every corner of their known world. Learn from their example, and you'll be able to revolutionize your own world: at home, in your community, and within the walls of your organization.

CHAPTER 1

A Six-Pack of Principles from a King and *the* King

GENESIS

When I was promoted from salesperson to sales manager, I thought that my new title officially announced to the world that I was a leader. I was wrong. In fact, I quickly learned three things:

1. A title doesn't make you a leader. It merely affords you an opportunity to become one.
2. As a leader, you don't automatically have followers, you have subordinates; how you act as a leader determines whether a subordinate ever becomes a follower.
3. Leadership is performance and not position. It is a choice you make, not a place where you sit.

Eager to excel in my new position, I worked hard on my job but I abused my body, swelling to 40 pounds overweight and earning my "new manager's merit badge"—an ulcer—in the process. To my credit, I was good at closing deals for my sales team, scheduling, forecasting, and writing daily memos for my bulging procedures manual. In a given day, I spent most of my time with "stuff," which I've since come to categorize as everything in my job that had nothing to do with people. In fact, I preferred the stuff over the people because I wasn't very good with people! I managed through intimidation, substituted rules for relationships, and had a hair-trigger temper that was a catalyst for creating a culture of fear. Although I had never attended a university, coworkers rightly claimed that I had a Master's Degree in Disempowerment and a Bachelor's in Bullying.

Then one day everything changed. Norm Albertson, the pastor of my church, stopped by my office and brought with him two leadership training programs by John Maxwell, a guy I had never heard of. One of the programs was on leadership priorities, and the other explained key differences between being a manager and being a leader—which I had wrongly thought were synonymous terms. Listening to Maxwell talk about leadership humbled me because I realized I was, at best, a ceremonial leader. All I had was a new title, which I wrongly assumed made me more competent! His teachings stirred up in me a desire to become a better leader. Frankly, I was tired of doing too much work by myself because I trusted no one else to share the load. I was also discouraged that I wasn't doing enough to help my people reach their potential. Perhaps what I was most excited about was that he said that the principles he taught were biblically based. This meant a lot to me because I had become a Christian at age 12 and had great respect for the Bible, even though I didn't spend a lot of time reading it at the time.

After reviewing the tapes several times, I began reading the Bible for business wisdom as well as for life wisdom. As a result, I changed my leadership style, priorities, and thinking. I began using the Bible as a filter to make decisions ranging from personnel to customer care issues. In the aftermath of implementing these changes, my career shifted from a slow shuffle up a steep staircase to an express elevator to the top.

As a student of the Bible, I have found that both success and failure leave clues, and you don't have to invent leadership principles to become more successful any more than you must suffer countless disappointments through personal trial and error to learn what doesn't work. Instead, you can learn from some of the best and worst leaders of all time who preceded you on this journey, as described in the Bible, and apply timeless, proven principles to improve every aspect of your organization. Think about it this way: the Bible is a slice of God's mind! How foolish do we have to be to continue to labor under our own intuition or to chase the fads of others in pursuit of greater success when the source of infinite wisdom is so readily available to us?

In this chapter, you'll learn from two of the best leaders in the Bible — a king and *the* King. You can certainly argue that there are additional or different leaders that I could have chosen to highlight in the following pages. And I would agree with you. In reality, there are too many to list, and enough lessons from their lives to fill volumes of books. Thus, I've chosen the two I believe you will gain the most benefit from in the shortest amount of time and who will best help you to begin running your business by THE BOOK.

Caution: Your natural tendency might be to use these principles to first try and fix the people or broken systems and strategies that surround you. That would be a serious error, because nothing is going to get much better in your organization until *you* do! You'll be relieved to know that, in this chapter, David and Jesus will offer six insightful steps (three each) on how you can make this happen.

By THE BOOK Blessing

Leadership is developed more than it is discovered. You work on it, and then it works for you.

DAVID

David was the second king of Israel, reigned for 40 years, and is considered to be its best ruler. His reign preceded the birth of Christ by approximately 1,000 years. Like many leaders, David made major mistakes in the midst of his enormous successes. We can learn from both.

9

DAVID'S CRITICAL SUCCESS FACTORS

Critical Success Factor #1: David Assumed the Traits of a Leader Before He Was in the Leadership Position

Over the years, I've heard this common chorus from non-management employees aspiring to be promoted: "Dave, I would like to be considered for the new management position that has opened up. I've been here a long time, I've been loyal, and I believe that I've earned a shot."

I would then ask them the following: "How many management books have you read, and how many leadership courses have you attended?" The predictable response was a sheepish and defensive, "None. I'm not a manager yet," to which I'd respond, "Wouldn't you agree that the best time to prepare yourself for the next step up is before you're in that position? After all, I don't want you to play a costly game of 'amateur hour' with our people. Learn about management before you're a manager. And while you're at it, show me that you can manage your own time, your own emotions, character choices, and discipline *now*, in the position you're currently in. Because, if you cannot manage yourself, how do you expect me to give you an opportunity to manage others?"

By THE BOOK Blessing

The first obligation of a leader is to grow. The process should start before you're in an official leadership position and continue for a lifetime once you're there.

BY THE BOOK LESSON IN LEADERSHIP

DAVID LED BEFORE HE HAD A TITLE

Historians estimate that David was a teenager when he fought Goliath. The Bible describes him as a "youth" when he decides to fight Goliath. He was willing to take action while King Saul and his professional soldiers quaked in their sandals as Goliath left his Philistine camp for 40 straight days to taunt the Israelis and challenge them to fight him. While others uttered excuses, David offered a solution. This is what leaders do. They begin thinking and acting like leaders before they're in a leadership position. And if they are already in a leadership position, they'll begin thinking and acting like the person who is in the next higher position to which they aspire would think and act.

If you want to own the company you work for, begin to think and act like an owner would think and act, even if you're currently sweeping floors and cleaning toilets. Allow me to relate a brief example of how this mindset works in the business arena.

While being given a tour of his operations by the CEO of a $300 million retail organization who had worked his way into ownership from the ground floor, I noticed that he'd stop, stoop, and scoop up every piece of trash in his path. When he noticed my amusement with his meticulous housekeeping he explained, "Most people think that I pick up the trash on this property because I own the company. What they don't realize is that I own the company because I've had a mindset from the day I started here that has never allowed me to walk past a piece of trash on this property without picking it up."

In some regards, not much has changed since the time of David. The largest corporations in the world emulate the Israeli army and King Saul by recognizing that their version of Goliath is a problem, but they take no action against the problem. A key aspect of leadership mandates that you move beyond problem-finding to solution-providing. In fact, a key difference between winners and whiners in any organization is that, although both groups point out problems and areas for improvement, the winners will also offer and implement remedies.

A second lesson we can learn from David's emergence as a leader is that he combated Goliath with more than just a great attitude as he repeated affirmations or by displaying the power of positive thinking. While all of these can add value, they are not a substitute for preparation and execution. Perhaps the most telling aspect of this well-known story is

11

found in 1 Samuel 17:40, where THE BOOK reports that, before facing the giant, David stopped by a brook and chose five smooth stones for battle. He didn't know if he'd need one or five; it was also rumored that Goliath had four brothers. Either way, he was ready! As a leader, you are expected to maintain a positive outlook and to maintain a healthy attitude. These are givens. A more relevant question becomes, "Do you have your five stones?" Have you prepared for the Goliath you're facing in the marketplace? Are you merely a wishful thinker, or have you earned the right to be legitimately optimistic by building a foundation under your organization that guarantees success?

By THE BOOK Blessing

The difference between optimism and wishful thinking is preparation! You must earn the right to be truly optimistic. A goal without a plan is mere hype.

Critical Success Factor #2: David Honored the Leader Above Him

An important aspect of leadership is being able to lead up. This means that you add value to, positively influence, and publicly support your leader. Leading up also requires that you don't try to change your leader. Rather, help him or her shore up their weaknesses by assuming duties that make both you and your leader more valuable. Honoring the leader above you is easier when the leader is moral, decent, and competent. But what if he or she is selfish, insecure, and filled with character flaws? Learn from David and his relationship with Saul.

By THE BOOK Blessing

Lead up well and you will move up fast.

King Saul's disobedience had caused God to instruct the prophet Samuel to anoint David as the next king of Israel, even while Saul was still reigning! In fact, David wouldn't assume the role of king for an estimated 15 years after he was anointed. During that time, he was intensely loyal to a jealous king who knew that his disfavor with God had numbered his days in power. As a result, and despite David's loyalty, Saul sought to kill him. Ironically, during Saul's quest to eliminate his rival, David had the opportunity to twice kill Saul, but would not do it because he believed that his decision, while expedient, would not be in alignment with God's will. David resolved that he would not take it upon himself to replace what God had put into place. Rather, he waited for God to dispense of Saul before fulfilling his destiny. In due time, God did His part, and David became the greatest king of Israel.

By THE BOOK Lesson in Leadership

Lead Up with Honor

You honor the leader above you by being publicly loyal to him or her, while confronting differences privately. You look for ways to make him or her look good. You volunteer to take on tasks that may not be within his or her strength zone, but are a better fit for your own abilities. You refrain from gossip and never conduct an "If I were in charge around here" conversation with subordinates. Even if you do not like the person, you respect his or her position and authority over you. If your leader performs illegal acts, then you must leave the organization. As Paul warned the Corinthians, "evil company corrupts good habits" (1 Corinthians 15:33). Trust God to deal with the person and to elevate you to a better place, either within or outside of the organization you're already in. Continuing to work for a corrupt leader because you profess that you want to change him or her is merely a rationalization for doing what is temporarily convenient rather than what is morally correct. Don't kid yourself; you can change yourself but you cannot change another human being.

Paul reinforced David's attitude toward authority more than 1,000 years later when he wrote to the Colossians while he was imprisoned in Rome by the same government authority that would one day kill him. Yet, even under those conditions, Paul had the right idea concerning authority:

"And whatever you do, do it heartily, as to the Lord and not to men, knowing that from the Lord you will receive the reward of the inheritance; for you serve the Lord Christ. But he who does wrong will be repaid for what he has done, and there is no partiality" (Colossians 3:23). It's important to keep this perspective and to render unto your leader as you would render unto God. You wouldn't stab God in the back, would you? Would you try to nudge God out of His position and maneuver yourself into it? (Satan tried this and was cast out of heaven along with one-third of the angels, who were his collaborators!) You wouldn't try to make God look bad or mock His rules or decisions, would you? If not, then don't do it to your leader, either. And neither should you listen to the voices of others who encourage you to do these things to your boss. David's men did the same thing to him by encouraging him to kill Saul when he had the chance. David refused to take God's matters into his own hands, and so should you.

The apostle Peter, when writing from Rome to all five provinces in Asia, said something similar in 1 Peter 2: 18–20:

> Servants, be submissive to your masters with all fear, not only to the good and gentle, but also to the harsh. For this is commendable, if because of conscience toward God one endures grief, suffering wrongfully. For what credit is it if, when you are beaten for your faults, you take it patiently? But when you do good and suffer, if you take it patiently, this is commendable before God.

One final thought in this regard: Don't worry if you're not getting enough credit or if you don't think anyone notices your good performance. God sees and He notices and, when you work according to His will, He will make things right.

I'd be remiss if I didn't include in this section at least a dash of biblical instruction for how leaders are to treat their people (leading down). Picking up where we left off in Colossians, in the very next verse, Paul creates the standard for how leaders should, in turn, treat their subordinates: *"Masters, give your bondservants what is just and fair, knowing that you also have a Master in heaven."*

14

In the 23 short verses in the book of Philemon, Paul offers instruction for how leaders should treat their workers, even when they go astray. Philemon was a wealthy friend of Paul who had helped him start the Colossian church in his own home. When Philemon's slave, Onesimus, ran away, Paul offered advice for how to deal with him when he returned. Hold him accountable? Yes, but see him first as a brother and then as an employee. In other words, although you may detest the performance, you must still love the performer.

By THE BOOK Blessing

Don't expect God to move you farther up the ladder until you're willing to hold steady the ladder for the leader whose authority you're currently under.

Critical Success Factor #3: David Confessed His Sins and Genuinely Repented When He Fell

Some of the most high-profile leaders of all time have failed morally. They've been caught in lies, adultery, and financial malfeasance. How quickly they are forgiven by followers—or not—often depends on their acceptance of responsibility, ability to admit their mistake, and repent for their error. Repenting is more than admitting that you've screwed up. It means that you change your ways and reconcile with those you've wronged. This action goes beyond mere words; it involves a change of heart. Perhaps this is why so many culprits are sorrier for the fact that they were caught than for the wrong they committed. In a nutshell, repentance requires humility before God and men.

By THE BOOK Blessing

The difference between regret and repentance is a heart condition.

David's Affair and Despair

David committed adultery with Bathsheba and then plotted to have her husband murdered. When confronted with his sin by the prophet Nathan,

David took a road we don't see many fallen leaders choose. He admitted it, he accepted responsibility, and he repented. In fact, Psalms 51, written by David, is a textbook example of how to repent. Those of you familiar with the life of David know that his repentance restored his relationship with the Lord, but it did not free him from the consequences of his sin. As foretold by Nathan, the son he conceived in adultery died, his own household would rise up against him, the sword would never depart from his house, and his women would lie publicly with strangers, in contrast to the sin he committed privately with Bathsheba. All of this happened. Don't mistake forgiveness with freedom from consequences. It is not.

BY THE BOOK LESSON IN LEADERSHIP

COME CLEAN QUICK!

Fast, forthright confessions of mistakes prevent hiccups from becoming cover-ups, and stop cover-ups from turning into conspiracies. Confessing your wrongs doesn't free you from consequences. However, it can diminish them, attract others to your side, and teach your team valuable lessons in how you expect them to respond in similar situations.

Avoid "I Did It . . . Buts"

Don't spoil a perfectly good apology or admission of an error with an excuse! "I admit it is my fault . . . but I was basing my decision on what you told me," or "I was wrong to say that. But you shouldn't have provoked me!" When you make a mistake, quickly come clean and don't attempt to rationalize your act! The longer you wait to admit what you did, the more suspect you'll become, and the faster your personal credibility will diminish. If you make the habit of quickly admitting your errors, you'll create a culture that encourages others to do the same and protect your good name as a leader. But if you whip out your black belt in blame to shift the focus off of you and onto something or someone else, you'll breed a brood of followers who become proficient at practicing professional victimhood every time something goes wrong.

By THE BOOK Blessing

When you make a mistake, admit it without justifying it; learn from it so that you don't repeat it; and understand that failing to do this quickly is another mistake in itself.

SUMMARY

David is the only person in the entire Bible described as being "a man after God's own heart." Learn from his successes and failures. Preparing yourself for your next leadership position before you're in that position, honoring the leaders and authority figures above you, and confessing mistakes and repenting when you fall short are three lessons that you can begin immediately internalizing in your life and career. They are also criteria you can use to measure others in your organization. In the next few pages, you'll learn three more lessons from the leadership of Jesus that will make up the "six-pack of principles" to internalize into your own leadership style as you begin to run your business by THE BOOK.

JESUS

Jesus is the ultimate leader who set the standard by which all other leaders must be measured against. In three short years of ministry, he laid the groundwork for a church destined to become the largest in the world.

JESUS' CRITICAL SUCCESS FACTORS

Critical Success Factor #1: Jesus Created Clarity of Vision, Values, and Performance Expectations

I've been told that the most helpful section of my leadership workshops is when I discuss the importance accountability plays in creating a high-performance culture. Although most leaders admit that they would like to build a high-accountability organization, they also confess that they've done a poor job of clearly establishing what is expected in terms of

17

performance metrics and behavioral standards in the first place. Because of this, the question in their quest for higher accountability becomes, "Accountable for what?"

By THE BOOK Blessing

Ambiguity is the enemy of accountability.

Throughout the Bible, God clearly spoke to His people. I can find no record of anyone ever saying to the Creator, "What was that? I didn't get it the first time." From the beginning of time, God made clear what was important to Him, and throughout His life on earth, Jesus continued this pattern by declaring His mission, vision, values, and what was expected of His followers. In fact, it can be said that the central theme of the Scriptures are the 49 general commands of Christ scattered throughout the Gospels. Many of them were based on Old Testament teachings. The letters of Paul and others speak at length about how to apply Christ's commands and weave them into your character and lifestyle. This is the essence of clarity: creating the standards, personally living them, and then teaching others to do likewise.

By THE BOOK Lesson in Leadership

Jesus Was Clear!

From the Sermon on the Mount (Matthew 5), to teaching disciples how to pray (Matthew 6), to the First and Second Great Commandments (Matthew 22), Jesus created clarity for performances and behaviors. Although His values sounded radical to many, they were not unclear!

Author Max De Pree declared that the first responsibility of a leader is to define reality. This being said, have you performed your first responsibility as a leader? Reality in your organization includes your vision, performance metrics, and behaviors. If you're not sure whether or not these issues are clear in your enterprise, then they probably are not. You either have them, or you don't. They're either in writing, or they're not. And if they don't positively influence employee behaviors on a daily basis, then they're impotent. Once you define reality, you must model it and talk about it repeatedly, just as Christ did. Point to those who live the standards, as Jesus did in acclaiming the widow who gave all she had (Luke 21:1–4), and confront or correct those who abuse or abandon the standards, as Christ did when His disciples argued about who was the greatest (Mark 10:35–45).

There are many aspects of your job that you can delegate. Defining reality isn't one of them! As the leader, you're expected to see more, to see sooner, and to see farther than followers. It is both your privilege and your responsibility to define reality in your organization, and it matters not if you lead 1 or 100,000. If your "reality" has gotten a bit cloudy, become conveniently forgotten, or was never created in the first place, then redefine it as soon as possible.

By THE BOOK Blessing

If you don't clearly define what you stand for, then you stand for nothing by default.

Critical Success Factor #2: Jesus Held Others Accountable for Results

While I was speaking overseas in a workshop on the topic of account-ability, an attendee remarked, "Holding others accountable is easier in your country because you have a more 'in-your-face' culture, but over here we're accustomed to acting as gentlemen. How do you recommend we hold our people accountable in a manner that fits our culture?" This gentleman's question is typical of the misunderstanding many people have concerning accountability. They believe that holding others accountable is harsh, mean, disrespectful, intimidating, or caustic. Unfortunately, this faulty grasp of how effective accountability works causes leaders to go light on the issue, inviting entitlement and mediocrity into their business culture as a result. THE BOOK instructs you to confront in love and also warns against the tendency and temptation to become prideful when you do confront. *"Brethren, if a man is overtaken in any trespass, you who are spiritual restore such a one in a spirit of gentleness, considering yourself lest you also be tempted"* (Galatians 1:1).

You can confront someone concerning his or her performance and be firm yet fair, and direct while being respectful. You can also be caring without coddling and empathic without condoning the offense. Read the first chapter of Galatians and you'll discover a textbook case in how to confront in love. Galatians is the only letter Paul wrote where he fails to affirm anyone or anything but jumps right into lovingly contend with the erring Galatian believers.

In the eighth chapter of John, we read how the Pharisees brought the woman caught in adultery to Jesus, reminded Him that Moses' law mandated that she be stoned, and asked His opinion in an effort to trap Him. The text indicates that Jesus said nothing but stooped down and wrote in the sand. When they continued asking Him, He stood up and said to them, "He who is without sin among you, let him throw a stone at her first," whereupon He stooped back down and wrote on the ground again. John related that those who witnessed this were convicted by their conscience and left one by one until none was left. When Jesus stood back up and was alone with the woman, He said to her, "Woman, where are those accusers of yours? Has no one condemned you?" She replied, "No one, Lord." And Jesus said to her, "Neither do I condemn you; go and sin no more."

This awesome lesson in accountability teaches three key points:

1. Confronting someone and holding them accountable doesn't mean that you have to condemn, lecture, or demean them.
2. After confrontation, you should always define a new performance expectation: "Go and sin no more."
3. You can prick the conscience of those who condemn, trash talk, and assail others by gently reminding them of their own shortcomings. Biblical scholars have long speculated what it was that Jesus twice

wrote in the sand. Many have suggested that He wrote the sins of the men who were accusing the woman. This would certainly explain them being convicted by their consciences and making a hasty exit!

By THE BOOK Blessing

The sole purpose of accountability and consequences is to improve performance. It is *not* to humiliate!

BY THE BOOK LESSON IN LEADERSHIP

USE THEM OR LOSE THEM!

The twenty-fifth chapter of Matthew relates one of THE BOOK's best lessons in accountability: Jesus' parable of the talents. Before talent meant aptitude, it meant money. It was the largest unit of measure in Greek accounting. To put the value of a talent in perspective, consider that a denarius was the measure for a fair day's wage and a talent was worth ten thousand day's wages! Suffice to say, Jesus was talking real money here.

As you read the paraphrased version of this story, consider how you can apply the tenets of accountability in your own organization.

A master was leaving town and brought together three of his servants to entrust with talents to invest during his absence. Custom dictated that when he returned from his journey, each servant would give an account of his results.

The master distributed the talents according to the servant's abilities: five talents to one, two to a second, and one talent to the third. After being gone a long while he returned to settle the accounts with his men. The servant who had received five talents doubled his money! The master was overjoyed and told him, "Well done, good and faithful servant; you were faithful over a few things, I will make you ruler over many things!" Next, the servant who had received two talents also reported that he had also doubled the master's money! The master was overjoyed once again and

21

> *offered the same affirmation and promise as he had to the first servant. Finally, the third servant came forth and explained that since he knew the master was a hard man, he was afraid he'd lose the money. Thus, he buried it into the ground and returned to his master the same talent he was given. Well, the master lost his cool, replying: "You wicked and lazy servant . . . you should have at least deposited the money into the bank so that I could collect interest. Take the talent from him, and give it to the one who has ten, because to everyone who has, more will be given, and he will have abundance; but from him who does not have, even what he has will be taken away. And cast the unprofitable servant out!"*

There are at least three lessons in accountability you can learn from the parable of the talents:

1. THE BOOK says that the master distributed the talents according to the ability of each servant. In other words, they didn't all get equal amounts. They got what they had earned and deserved based on past performance. This ethic has disappeared from many modern business cultures, in which entitled employees expect enrichment because they show up rather than step up.
2. The worker who produces the best results should be given more opportunities and resources, even if it is at the expense of a poor performer who doesn't have as much. Don't weaken the strong to strengthen the weak! Rather, leverage the strong, and weed out the weak performers.
3. In the parable, Jesus did not condemn the master for dealing firmly with the servant. Rather, he had the harshest words for he who had an opportunity but failed to do anything with it. After all, the master clearly established the expectation. The servant knew what he was expected to do, but didn't do it.

Jesus was tougher on those who knew better and were in positions of authority, and you should be also. This is why He reserved some of his most critical statements for the Pharisees, scribes, and lawyers.

Throughout His life, Jesus only held people accountable for what they had been given. He never did and never will hold others accountable for what they didn't have: knowledge, opportunities, resources, position, and the like. Perhaps this is why Luke quotes Jesus as saying:

> And that servant who knew his master's will and did not prepare himself or do according to his will, shall be beaten with many stripes. But he who did not know, yet committed things deserving of stripes, shall be beaten with few. For everyone to whom much is given, from him much will be required; and to whom much has been committed, of him they will ask the more. (Luke 18:47–48)

This standard may be what prompted James, Jesus' half-brother, to write in his epistle a few years after Jesus' resurrection:

> My brethren, let not many of you become teachers, knowing that we shall receive a stricter judgment. (James 3:1)

I'd be remiss if I didn't conclude the lessons on accountability with a reminder that without applying the first critical success factor of Jesus' leadership discussed in this chapter—creating clarity of mission, vision, values, and performance expectations—then accountability is impossible.

By THE BOOK Blessing

Gray areas invite complacency, entitlements, and chaos. In a high-accountability culture, there is right and wrong; success and failure; winning and losing.

Critical Success Factor #3: Jesus Served Others

In one of my leadership workshops, I present 20 differences between management and leadership mindsets, and their impact on performance. The first difference that I explain is, "Managers want to be served, whereas leaders serve others." I go on to explain that *serving* is not a warm and fuzzy term that is out of touch with the realities of running an organization. Serving means that you add value to others rather than wait for them to add value to you. Serving acknowledges that, as a leader, you need your people more than they need you. You serve people by setting clear expectations for them, giving them honest feedback, training them, holding them accountable, and offering to them increased latitude, discretion, and opportunities. Serving also acknowledges that the good of the team must come before your own comfort level or agenda.

Leaders serve their people by displaying the Four Cs: character, competence, compassion, and consistency. The Four Cs earn a depth of loyalty from followers that command-and-control pretenders-with-titles can only dream about. Serving puts into motion a reciprocal cycle—the more you serve, the more others want to help and serve you in return. Even a poor leader can buy a follower's hands with a paycheck, but servant leaders earn their hearts and heads as well. Serving is a mindset. It reminds you that leadership is about performance, and not about position. Serving helps you cultivate humility. It puts into perspective that, despite your lofty title, you're no better than anyone else. Serving helps you connect with others. It touches the core of their hearts before demanding the sweat of their brow.

Jesus was ready, willing, and able to serve. From the seemingly small things—like at a wedding feast He attended with his disciples in Canaan when His mother, Mary, told him, "They have no wine." Even though His time hadn't yet come, He accommodated mom's request and gave Mary the opportunity to preach her one and only sermon recorded in THE BOOK, when she instructed the servants: "Whatever He says to you, do it." Then there were major acts like healing the lame, raising the dead, casting out demons, restoring sight to the blind, and feeding hungry multitudes. He served His men by spending three years teaching, mentoring, and pouring His life into theirs, and performed the ultimate act of service: suffering torture and death on a cross so that others might live. Very importantly however, Jesus *looked* for ways to serve; He didn't sit in a temple waiting for others to come to Him. Jesus managed by walking around long before Tom Peters wrote about it in *In Search of Excellence*. Jesus knew that you can't serve well if you're static, stale, or immobile. You must be around people to serve people and must look for ways to connect with them rather than wait for them to connect with you.

By THE BOOK Blessing

If you think that your people are there to serve you, versus you serving them, you're not a leader; you're a tyrant.

By THE BOOK Lesson in Leadership

THE BOOK relates several instances of Jesus' disciples arguing about which of them was the greatest. (Does this sound like the dialogue in the corridors after your weekly management meeting?) In the tenth chapter of Mark, Jesus sets the record straight concerning greatness:

> Yet it shall not be so among you; but whoever desires to become great among you shall be your servant. And whoever of you desires to be first shall be slave of all. For even the Son of Man did not come to be served, but to serve, and to give His life a ransom for many. (Mark 10:43–45)

Please note two key points in this passage:

1. Jesus didn't knock trying to be great. He merely offered a recipe for making it happen: serving others.
2. Jesus defined His own mission as not coming to be served, but to serve. This is particularly important when you read Romans 8:29, where Paul writes that we are called to be conformed to the image of Jesus. In other words, we are to serve as He served.

Foxhole Leaders Are Servants

Foxhole friends are those you want on your side when the going gets tough. You can count on them. They've got your back. When you're coming under attack and hunkered down in a foxhole, you need someone at your right hand with the Four Cs of character, competence, compassion, and consistency. The characteristics required to be labeled as a foxhole friend attract loyalty from others, and in leadership this is essential. Foxhole friends will pay a price to be with you and to be a part of what you're doing. Considering this, would your people classify you as a foxhole leader? Can they count on your character, competence, compassion, and consistency, even when things get tough? Do they trust you to put their own welfare ahead of your own comfort level? Do you have followers who because of your leadership style are willing to trouble themselves for you, sacrifice for you, take heat for you, or maybe even take a bullet for you? Jesus did. And it wasn't because He got lucky. Rather, He lived a life of integrity, competence, and service that drew others to Him. Jesus was such an effective foxhole leader that even 2,000 years later His followers are willing to die for Him, and they often do.

One of the greatest tests of a leader's effectiveness is whether or not he or she still influences people after his or her departure. Although THE BOOK doesn't say much about the fate of Jesus' disciples and closest followers in the early years of Christianity, early church historians like Eusebius and Josephus tell us plenty. If judging the sacrifices others are willing to make for your sake is a key indicator of your success as a leader, you will be impressed with what is next. While John died of natural causes in A.D. 98, the fates of the rest of the 12, who continued to spread the message of their leader, as well as a few key others, are as follows:

- James the apostle, brother of John, was beheaded A.D. 44.
- Philip the apostle was stoned and crucified A.D. 54.
- Matthew the apostle was beheaded in Ethiopia A.D. 70.
- James the apostle, son of Alphaeus, was stoned in Syria A.D. 60.
- Matthias, the apostle who took Judas' place, was stoned in Jerusalem A.D. 70.
- Andrew the apostle was crucified in Patras A.D. 70.

- Mark, author of the gospel bearing his name, was dragged to death in Alexandria, Egypt A.D. 64.
- Peter the apostle was crucified in Rome A.D. 69.
- Paul the apostle was beheaded in Rome the same day Peter was crucified A.D. 69.
- Judas, also known as Thaddeus the apostle, was killed by arrows/javelin in Armenia A.D. 70.
- Bartholomew, also known as Nathanael the apostle, was skinned alive and crucified in Armenia A.D. 70.
- Thomas the apostle was tortured, baked in an oven, and stuck through with spears in India A.D. 70.
- Luke, author of the gospel bearing his name and Acts, was hanged in Greece A.D. 93.
- Simon the Zealot the apostle was sawed in half in the Middle East A.D. 74.
- James, half-brother of Jesus, was thrown from a building, stoned, and beaten in Jerusalem A.D. 62.
- Timothy, Paul's right-hand man and the Bishop of Ephesus, was stoned and beaten in Ephesus A.D. 80.

Your People Would Rather See a Sermon Than Hear One!
One of the most well-known stories of Jesus' servant leadership is when He washed the disciples' feet, the night of the Last Supper—less than 24 hours before His torture and murder. For three years, Jesus had preached and lived servant-based leadership, yet His own disciples continued to argue about greatness and jockey for position. Rather than give a final lecture on serving others, Jesus decided to show, again, what good performance looks like. But this time would be even more dramatic because washing feet was such a despicable and degrading act that a master could not even order his slave to do it. In biblical times, there was no part of the body—and I do mean *no* part—that was more filthy, stinky, and disgusting than one's feet! Read the account in the thirteenth chapter of John with a servant leader's eyes.

27

Here are three lessons that should stand out:

1. Jesus didn't just talk about good performance. He demonstrated what it looked like because He knew that seeing a sermon is more impacting to a follower than hearing one.
2. Jesus didn't delegate this task of servant-hood, nor did He run an ad in the *Jerusalem Times* seeking a good foot-washer. He did the deed Himself.
3. Jesus washed the feet of Judas—the man He knew would betray Him. He didn't only serve the people He knew would serve Him.

By THE BOOK Blessing

You can't serve others until you first die to yourself. There is no "I" in servant.

SHINE THE LIGHT

As he lost election after election, Abraham Lincoln was reported to have declared, "I will prepare myself and some day my chance will come." It did come for Lincoln and, fortunately, for the United States, he had forged, during his down times, the character and temperament to effectively lead the nation through the Civil War.

Waiting for your next, bigger, more exciting leadership opportunity can be painful, but it needn't be if you use the time wisely and maintain the proper perspective. You can start by following the examples of Lincoln and David, and work diligently to assume and develop the traits necessary for your next leadership opportunity before it presents itself. Here are some thoughts on converting "waiting time" into "prime time."

1. A study of the Scriptures reveals that those God used greatly were often prepared for those exploits during periods of solitude, quietness, and obscurity: Moses, David, Joseph, Elijah, and John the

Baptist. Sustained periods of preparation fuel the future effectiveness of great leaders.[1]

2. Becoming more precedes doing more. The "becoming" must happen first and includes increasing in maturity, discipline, humility, knowledge, competence, righteousness, and focus. To do more than you've done, and to get more than you've got, you must first become more than you are.

3. You can't advance spiritually when you're immersed in busyness. Becoming a deeper leader, capable of accomplishing greater things, requires an incubation period that includes solitude, study, and reflection.

4. During your waiting period, don't promote yourself, drop hints, or push yourself to the front. Let others do this. Better yet, let *God* do this. Self-promotion is neither necessary nor attractive. If you're truly gifted, people will find you. During the times when no one seems to notice you or your contributions, practice the discipline of becoming more valuable so that you can add more value.[2]

5. Exceptional work and achievement is often preceded by extended waiting. Don't despise the wait that adds depth to your life. Moving fast in order to give the impression that you're more accomplished than you actually are is both dangerous and delusional. Speed can disguise the fact that you lack the foundation of character and competence necessary to justify additional responsibility and opportunity. Sadly, advancing quickly without a foundation can render you as shallow, and shallow lives impact no one and add value to nothing.

6. During your waiting time, remain obedient to God. Don't rush God or take shortcuts anchored in your own wisdom. Trust God, and you'll obey Him. Obedience always stimulates growth.[3]

7. A life marked by depth and steeped in preparation can only be cultivated in protracted periods of feeling like you're in "no man's land" and getting nowhere fast. Cherish these times, because in them you plant and cultivate the seeds that position you for your next leadership harvest.

Summary

Jesus was perfect. We're not. But we become complete as we conform ourselves to His image and imitate every aspect of His life. Lead in a manner so that your followers see less of you and more of Him. Pray that you will see the way He sees, hear the way He hears, think the way He thinks, love what He loves, and hate what He hates.

Revelation

I've presented six essential traits to incorporate into your leadership style. The chances are good that you knew these things before you read them in the preceding pages. But knowing isn't the point. *Doing* is what counts! By taking the time to do the following exercises, you will demonstrate a commitment that affirmations alone could never accomplish and create personal momentum to help you begin leading by THE BOOK.

ACTION EXERCISE

Six Lessons in Leadership from a King and *the* King

Considering the six principles presented:

1. Which offers you the greatest opportunity to improve your own leadership style?

   _____

2. Which are your strongest?

   _____

3. Which are your weakest?

   _____

4. List at least one step you can take to improve each of the six traits listed:
   A. How can you assume the traits of the next position to which you aspire?
   B. How can you better honor the leader/authority over you?

C. What action/behavior must you admit and repent from?
D. How can you improve clarity in your organization?
E. How can you improve accountability in your organization and your personal methods for holding others accountable?
F. What mindset must you assume or actions can you take to assume a more genuine servant's role as a leader?

Use the six previous questions as a coaching tool to improve the leadership style of your key leaders.

CHAPTER 2

Four Mandates to Maximize Your Time

GENESIS

In Chapter 1, I mentioned that one of the John Maxwell programs given to me by my pastor concerned priorities. Maxwell presented the Pareto Principle, which, among other things, teaches that 20 percent of your activities bring 80 percent of your results. This was news to me! I thought priorities were the loudest and most pressing emergencies of the moment. As a result, I left my calendar wide open in anticipation of the crises I'd deal with each day, without realizing that doing so guaranteed I would spend most days being chased by what was urgent. After watching the priorities program, I humbly recognized that if ignorance were truly bliss, I should have been a lot happier than I was at the time!

Three principles of time management I've embraced and implemented since learning the Pareto Principle many years ago are: (1) It's not the hours or days you put in that make you effective; it's what you put *in* the hours and days. (2) Putting second things first is one of the key reasons why most people never reach their goals. Peter Drucker's sage advice still rules: "First things first and last things not at all," as does Stephen Covey's: "The main thing is to keep the main thing the main thing." (3) The primary objective of time management is not to get all of your work done. Rather, it is to get the *right* things done!

For decades, speaker Jim Rohn has taught the principle: "Don't spend major time on minor things, and don't spend minor time on the major things." I used to do the opposite of what he recommends, primarily because I never identified what my priorities were in the first place. Thank God I've learned three priority principles since those early career days when I engaged in time management amateur hour. They are: (1) Your priorities are not the good things you do each day; they are the great things. After all, many of the tasks you may engage in each day are good, rather than bad. Thus, from the good you must identify and execute the great first. (2) The only way you are likely to engage in your priorities is to schedule them. In fact, it is far more effective to schedule your priorities than to prioritize your schedule. (3) Priorities change, so you must remain flexible.

I also discovered that each day I was likely to temporarily get off track with time management, but the key was to recognize it fast and make an immediate adjustment. In the real world there are emergencies, interruptions, and distractions that take you off your game. The key is not to stay off, because the longer you work outside the discipline of priorities, the less effective you are.

As I read THE BOOK, I realized that God was and is the ultimate time manager. After all, in the tenth chapter of Joshua he made the sun stand still, and in the twentieth chapter of 2 Kings, He actually made time go backward! It's not likely you'll ever pull off these miracles, but you can become far better at making each of your days a masterpiece — getting *from* each day, rather than through it. Following are four time management mandates that will help you become a better steward of one of God's greatest gifts: your time.

By THE BOOK Blessing

You're never likely to get all of your work done because in a growing organization there is always an infinite amount of work to do. Thus, focus on getting the *right* things done first, and stop doing the wrong things well and often.

FOUR MANDATES FOR MAXIMIZING TIME

TIME MAXIMIZATION MANDATE #1: GET IN YOUR ZONE AND STAY THERE

For the purposes of time management, consider your personal zone to be that area of your own responsibilities in which time invested brings the greatest return of results. Normally, this is an area or areas where you can use your strengths, your talents, and, as a result, accomplish the most in the least amount of time. For instance, you may have great people skills. When you're motivating, training, and mentoring people, you're in your zone. The problem arises when you spend so much time with "stuff" that you have no time for people! You may work long and hard but are unable to maximize your time because you're not laboring in your highest return area. In fact, every time you step out of your zone, you lose some of your effectiveness. Stay out of it for too long or too often, and you'll lose your impact as a leader. During the course of a day, you're likely to be pulled out of your zone often. Getting back into it as soon as possible is essential if you wish to remain ultimately productive.

By THE BOOK Blessing

Part of the leadership maturation process is being able to look in the mirror and know what you're good at, as well as acknowledge what you're unfit to do, and to be at peace with both realities.

Go for "Complementary," Not Clones!

It is vital that you build a team with complementary skills and talents, so that you can spend enough time in your zone. You simply must surround yourself with people who are good at the things you are not. When they stay in their zone and you remain in yours, the entire organization continues to move forward. This is why Stephen Covey said, "The job of a leader is to build a complementary team, where every strength is made effective and each weakness is made irrelevant." Foolishly, many leaders do the opposite and assemble a team of people in their own image, a cache of clones that cannot complement one another, creating serious weaknesses and blind spots throughout the organization.

By THE BOOK Lesson in Leadership

None of Us Alone Is as Effective as All of Us Together!

Paul shared great wisdom concerning the importance of a diversity of talents, and the vital role each plays for the good of the whole team when he wrote in 1 Corinthians 12:17–26:

> If the whole body were an eye, where would be the hearing? If the whole were hearing, where would be the smelling? But now God has set the members, each one of them, in the body just as He pleased. And if they were all one member, where would the body be?
>
> But now indeed there are many members, yet one body. And the eye cannot say to the hand, "I have no need of you;" nor again, the head to the feet, "I have no need of you." No, much rather, those members of the body which seem to be weaker are necessary. And those members of the body which we think to be less honorable, on these we bestow the greatest honor; and our unpresentable parts have greater modesty but our presentable parts have no need. But God composed the body, having given greater honor to that part which lacks it, that there should be no schism in the body, but that the

members should have the same care for one another. And if one member suffers, all the members suffer with it; or if one member is honored, all the members rejoice with it.

In 1 Corinthians 12:4–11 is a great analogy of how complementary gifts benefit the whole church. This same explanation applies equally well to demonstrate the benefit of a complementary team to your own enterprise:

There are diversities of gifts, but the same Spirit. There are differences of ministries, but the same Lord. And there are diversities of activities, but it is the same God who works all in all. But the manifestation of the Spirit is given to each one for the profit of all: for to one is given the word of wisdom through the Spirit, to another the word of knowledge through the same Spirit, to another faith by the same Spirit, to another gifts of healings by the same Spirit, to another gifts of miracles, to another prophecy, to another discerning of spirits, to another different kinds of tongues, to another the interpretation of tongues. But one and the same Spirit works all these things, distributing to each one individually as He wills.

By THE BOOK Blessing

"I can do what you can't do. You can do what I can't do. Together, we can do great things."

—Mother Teresa

The "Twelve's" Two-Task Zone

The Book of Acts tells of how the 12 apostles decided that the only way that they could accomplish more was by doing fewer tasks, and spending more time on a handful of essential endeavors:

Now, in those days, when the number of the disciples was multiplying, there arose a complaint against the Hebrews by the Hellenists because their widows were neglected in daily distribution. Then the 12 summoned the multitude of disciples and said:

It is not desirable that we should leave the word of God and serve tables. Therefore, brethren, seek out from among you seven men of good reputation, full of the Holy Spirit and wisdom, whom we may appoint over this business; but we will give ourselves continually to prayer and to the ministry of the word.

And the saying pleased the whole multitude. And they chose Stephen, a man full of faith and the Holy Spirit, and Philip, Prochorus, Nicanor, Timon, Parmenas, and Nicolas, a proselyte from Antioch, whom they set before the apostles; and when they had prayed, laid hands on them.

Then the word of God spread, and the number of disciples multiplied greatly in Jerusalem, and a great many of the priests were obedient to the faith. (Acts 6:1–7)

Note four key lessons from this passage:

1. The leaders did not say that the work they were doing was beneath them, but that it was not desirable that they leave the great work to do the good work.
2. The 12 apostles delegated thoughtfully, and to men who had the right qualifications. From among many possibilities, they chose the best seven.
3. The 12 had narrowed their focus down to a two-priority zone: continuous prayer and ministry of the word.
4. Once this realignment of priorities was accomplished, results increased dramatically.

In fact, THE BOOK records that two of the chosen "waiters" went on to do great things: Stephen proclaiming the gospel so boldly that he became the first recorded Christian martyr (Acts 6:8–7:60), and Philip evangelizing and bringing revival to Samaria.

BY THE BOOK LESSON IN LEADERSHIP

DO LESS AND ACCOMPLISH MORE!

Some managers brag about being a jack-of-all-trades. However, they never complete the old cliché and admit that in the process, they have become a master of none. Although it is beneficial to *know* a little about a lot of things, it is not wise to *do* a little of a lot of things because every time you do, you step out of your zone. In fact, one of the paradoxes of time management is that you should do less and accomplish more. I'm not referring to doing less work per se but spending more time on fewer tasks — the zone tasks — and gaining greater results in the process.

By THE BOOK Blessing

Perhaps the three most important words as relates to time management are: *narrow your focus!* Make the shift from doing many things well to doing fewer things with greater excellence.

TIME MAXIMIZATION MANDATE #2: GIVE UP TO GO UP

The second principle for becoming a better time steward is to decide what you must give up in order to go up. In other words, now that you've identified and committed to your priorities, what must you stop doing to ensure that you complete your priorities each day?

I recall attending a management training class that taught about priorities. The instructor suggested that, as a manager, I could gain a great return on my time by making one-on-one coaching sessions with my team members a daily practice. I agreed with his assessment, returned to the workplace, and failed to conduct a single one-on-one! As is the case so often, I knew what to do, but I wasn't doing it. Part of the reason was that I failed to schedule them. Another mistake is that I never decided what I would stop doing so that I would have time to conduct the one-on-ones. As a result, I was more exasperated in the wake of the training class than I was before I attended, because I now knew what my priorities were but was disgusted with myself because I wasn't doing them.

By THE BOOK Blessing

Adding tasks to your "to-do" list is not the key to becoming more effective. First, you must begin a "stop doing" list. You must decide what you will give up so that you can go up.

By THE BOOK Lesson in Leadership

Father-in-Law Knows Best!

You're unlikely to ever become a great time manager if your primary objective is to determine how much work you can do personally. What's more important is that you learn to get work done through others. Frankly, what you can accomplish on your own is finite, but what you can achieve through a well-directed team of competent coworkers is nearly limitless. If you don't make the vital transition from doing it all yourself to accomplishing more through others, you'll be like an octopus on roller skates: lots of movement but very little forward progress.

Moses was 80 years old before God called him to lead His people out of Egypt, but he still had plenty to learn about time management. In the eighteenth chapter of Exodus, Moses' father-in-law, Jethro, gives his son-in-law a lesson in knowing what *not* to do, as Moses was personally settling the disputes among his two-million-member flock! Jethro's advice is leadership gold:

> And so it was, on the next day, that Moses sat to judge the people; and the people stood before Moses from morning until evening. So when Moses' father-in-law saw all that he did for the people, he said, "What is this thing that you are doing for the people? Why do you alone sit, and all the people stand before you from morning until evening?"
>
> And Moses said to his father-in-law, "Because the people come to me to inquire of God, and I judge between one and another; and I make known the statutes of God and His laws."
>
> So Moses' father-in-law said to him, "This thing that you do is not good. Both you and these people who are with you will surely wear yourselves out. For this thing is too much for you; you are not able to perform it by yourself. Listen now to my voice; I will give you counsel, and God will be with you: Stand before God for the people, so that you may bring the difficulties to God. And you shall teach them the statutes and the laws, and show them the way in which they must walk and the work they must do. Moreover, you shall select from all the people, able men, such as fear God ... And let them judge the people at all times. Then it will be that every great matter they shall bring to you, but every small matter they themselves will judge. So it will be easier for you, for they will bear the burden with you." (Exodus 18:13–22)

By THE BOOK Blessing

To move to the next level of leadership, you must stop confusing activity with accomplishment and cease doing the wrong things well. When you are seduced by the trivial, you disengage from the essential.

41

By THE BOOK Lesson in Leadership

Repeat After Me: "No."

William Gladstone once advised, "Wise is he who invests no effort into matters for which he is not suited. And wiser is he still, from amongst the things he does well, resolutely chooses to do the best." If you endeavor to become a great time steward, you must learn to say "no" to low-return tasks; "no" to procrastination; "no" to interruptions; and "no" to the people who have nothing to do and insist on doing it with you!

Early in His ministry, Jesus had just given an all-star performance and the crowd wanted an encore. Should He stay or should He move on? That was the question. Because His ministry was just getting started, it must have been tempting to linger and mingle and wow the throngs one last time before traveling to the next stop. But Jesus knew his priorities and focused on them like a laser. He didn't allow what was good to get in the way of what was best. He knew what He'd have to give up in order to go up, as Mark tells us early on in his gospel:

> At evening, when the sun had set, they brought to Him all who were sick and those who were demon possessed. And the whole city was gathered together at the door. Then He healed many who were sick with various diseases and cast out many demons; and He did not allow the demons to speak, because they knew Him.
>
> Now in the morning, having risen a long while before daylight, He went out and departed to a solitary place; and there He prayed. And Simon, and those who were with Him searched for Him. When they found Him, they said to Him, "Everyone is looking for You."
>
> But He said to them, "Let us go into the next towns, that I may preach there also, because for this purpose I have come forth." (Mark 1:38)

Don't let easy things, hard things, urgent things, or enjoyable things get in the way of the "first" things as you move toward your goals!

By THE BOOK Blessing

"No" keeps you in control of your time, priorities, and progress. It is a time steward's best friend.

TIME MAXIMIZATION MANDATE #3: KNOW GOD'S WILL FOR YOUR LIFE

My observation has been that most people—Christians included—who waste not only days, but decades, have no idea what God's will is for their life. As a result they dart, dabble, or drift with no sense of direction from one whim to the next, trusting their gut more than God. Although you're unlikely to ever hear this question in a secular time management seminar, you must ask yourself this life-changing question: "How can I manage and maximize a day, much less my life, without knowing what God's will for my life is?" The answer is, you cannot.

By THE BOOK Blessing

You won't determine God's will for your life by sending up a "flare prayer" when you need Him to bail you out of a mess your own will has gotten you into. To discover His will you must first lose your own.

Jesus' Mission Statement

The Bible never reports that Jesus had trouble making a decision. Nor are there conversations recorded in which He gathered His disciples and asked, "Okay guys, what should we do next?" This is because Jesus knew His mission, and that alone made it easy to say "no" to the wrong things and "yes" to what was right. From where did He get his mission? John 6:38–40 explains:

For I have come down from heaven, not to do My own will, but the will of Him who sent Me. This is the will of the Father who sent Me, that of all He has given Me I should lose nothing, but should raise it up on the last day. And this is the will of Him who sent Me, that everyone who sees the Son and believes in Him may have everlasting life; and I will raise him up at the last day.

By THE BOOK Lesson in Leadership

If It's Not in the Will, It's a Waste!

Paul understood the importance of knowing God's will when he wrote from prison to the Ephesians: "*Therefore, be careful how you walk, not as unwise men but as wise, making the most of your time, because the days are evil. So then, do not be foolish, but understand what the will of the Lord is*" (Ephesians 5:15–17). Paul suggests that without knowing God's will you are likely to engage in evil, destructive, or foolish pursuits, just as those who are categorized as "unwise" do. It is your responsibility to be careful with regard to your use of time, because how you use time is a clear issue of your foolishness or wisdom, obedience or rebellion. To make the most of your time, you must have a clear understanding of what God's will really is. Just as "whatever is not of faith is sin" (Romans 14:23), so anything that is other than the will of God is a waste of time.

Two Parts God, One Part You

Discerning God's personal will for you is easier if you understand His providential and moral will.

1. Providential will: God's providential will includes things THE BOOK says that He's going to do regardless. For example, sending Christ to earth, Judgment Day, and raising up a nation of His chosen people are things He has done and will do—period. You

don't have to pray for these things to happen; they are not contingent upon faith or obedience, and there is nothing man can do to stop them. God uses men and women like Abraham and Mary to fulfill His providential will. The more you understand God's providential will, the easier it will be to determine what His will for your life is.

2. Moral will: God's moral will concerns commands—the "thou shalts" and "thou shalt nots" found throughout THE BOOK. "Should I lie or tell the truth?" "Should I pay my taxes, speed, commit adultery, or gossip?" The more you know about God's moral will, the easier it is to discern his personal will for your life.

3. Personal will: "Should I go into debt or not?" "Do I take this job or that one?" "Should I hire Fred or Harry?" Here is a key point concerning God's providential, moral, and personal will for your life: the more familiar you are with the first part, and the more obedient you are to the second, the easier it is to discover the third. In fact, every decision you make will intersect with one of God's principles. The more that you know about these principles, the easier it is to know God's will in any situation.

By THE BOOK Blessing

Students of THE BOOK are the best decision makers because they have a holy filter through which to strain their deliberations.

Commitment Precedes Understanding

Most people never get a handle on God's will for their lives because they want to understand what it is first and then decide if they'll commit to it. But that's not how it works! You can't try to understand and then decide to commit; you must *commit* first, and then you begin to *understand* as God reveals the right course to you. If you're unclear on what it is that you should be doing, where you should be doing it, or with whom you should be doing it, then you've probably had the commitment/understanding

45

sequence backward. If this is the case, then you must ponder the following five points:

1. God doesn't reveal His will for deliberation but for participation.
2. You'll hear from God when you get to the point where you say, "I don't care what it is; the answer is 'yes!'"
3. The problem is never that God doesn't want to reveal His will to you. The problem is either that you don't commit or you don't follow through once He does.
4. God reveals His will to you gradually so that you draw closer to Him daily and depend on yourself less. God's goal for you seeking His will is that you come to know *Him* better.
5. Appreciate the importance of "all" in Proverbs 3:5–6: "*Trust in the Lord with all your heart, and lean not on your own understanding. In all your ways acknowledge Him, and He shall direct your paths.*"

The *all* is the key because if you want God to reveal His will to you, then you must trust and put Him first in every area of your life and not just the realm where you're seeking His guidance.

By THE BOOK Blessing

God invented communication and is the world's best communicator! He wants you to know His will even more than you want to know it.

Time Maximization Mandate #4: Pursue the Gifts You Have, Not the Gifts You Want!

I can't sing; in fact I shouldn't! It is not my talent. Thus, it would be a horrible misuse of time to invest my energies trying to improve my voice. The fact that I enjoy singing doesn't change this. Many things you enjoy doing may bring little or no value to your organization. What's essential is that you pursue the talents that you do have and not those that you want.

Because I have no gift for singing doesn't mean that I could never get any better at it, but it does mean that I'll never be great at it because excellence is impossible without talent. Certainly, I could hire a voice coach to teach me techniques that make the sounds that fall out of my mouth less offensive. This coach could prop me up with training that would limit the damage I do to others with my voice. But the coach won't help me become talented in an area in which I have no talent. The coach can't put inside of me what God left out. She can only help draw out what is there, which in my case doesn't amount to much.

Being a good time steward means that you spend your time developing and using the gifts that God gave you—the abilities that will bring the greatest fulfillment to you personally and the most significant return to your organization.

By THE BOOK Blessing

Whenever you invest time in your gift zone, you accelerate results. This is because it is easier to build upon a foundation that is already established than to erect a foundation from scratch on the quicksand of mediocrity.

Use Your Own Armor

The seventeenth chapter of 1 Samuel explains that, when Saul was counseling David concerning fighting Goliath, the king clothed David in his own armor, put a bronze helmet on his head, and also clothed him with a protective coat. Verses 39 through 40 tell what happened next: "*David fastened his sword to the armor and tried to walk, for he had not tested them. And David said to Saul, 'I cannot walk with these, for I have not tested them.'*" So David took them off.

Then he took his own staff in his hand, and he chose for himself five smooth stones from the brook and put them in a pouch that he had, and his sling was in his hand. And he drew near to the Philistine.

David couldn't do his job by trying to be someone he was not or by using gifts foreign to him. Nor can you. David took his own staff, his own pouch, and his own sling into battle and you must do the same. Be the best that you can be with your own unique gifts. Don't waste your precious time or opportunities acting like someone else. Get in your zone, armed with your gifts, and stay there!

47

By THE BOOK Lesson in Leadership

God Will Maximize Your Strengths

Throughout THE BOOK, God uses the unique skills, gifts, and talents of men and women to help them accomplish great things, and nowhere does He encourage that they try to become something they are not in these regards. Both Moses and David had shepherding skills that God greatly leveraged in their leadership roles. Matthew knew numbers and money. As a result, his gospel has more written about financial matters than the others. Luke was a historian and physician. Subsequently, the book bearing his name presents the most chronological of the four gospels, and his gives the only account of Jesus sweating drops of blood in Gethsemane, a condition doctors recognize today as hematohidrosis. Ezra used his teaching and writing skills to make the words of God understandable and authored several Old Testament books. God leveraged the same zeal, drive, and commitment Saul used to persecute Christians to further the gospel after Saul's conversion to Paul. In all of these cases, God held His people accountable for what they had, not the things they didn't have. Because God doesn't change, you can be assured that the same holds true for you today.

By THE BOOK Blessing

You can make each day a masterpiece as you narrow your focus and work within the discipline of priorities as dictated by your talents. Then delegate, automate, outsource, or just stop doing everything else!

What Are My Talents . . . and What If They're Not Great?
Talents are gifts from God. They are a special wiring—an ability that allows you to do something easily that someone else finds difficult. Not only that, but you can do it well nearly every time. However, talent is only potential; it is not a guarantee of success. Talent doesn't arrive

fully developed; it must be cultivated. Regardless of how minor or insignificant you may believe your talents to be, God would beg to differ with you. He would remind you that when you give Him what you have—even when it doesn't seem like much—He can do great things with it. Consider two examples:

1. Exodus 4:2–5: "*So the Lord said to Moses, 'What is that in your hand?' He said, 'A rod.' And He said, 'Cast it on the ground.' So Moses cast it on the ground, and it became a serpent; and Moses fled from it. Then the Lord said to Moses, 'Reach out your hand and take it by the tail' (and he reached out his hand and caught it, and it became a rod instantly in his hand), that they may believe that the Lord God of their fathers, the God of Abraham, the God of Isaac, and the God of Jacob has appeared to you.*"

   When Moses was obedient to God and gave Him what he held in his hand, God transformed it into something of great power. God would work miracles through that rod as Moses appealed to Pharaoh, to turn rivers to blood, to bring plagues of locusts and darkness, to part the Red Sea, and more. And in case you believe you're too old to get in your zone, use your gifts, and become more effective in your endeavors, then consider that Moses was 80 before he turned his rod over to God.

2. Matthew 6:8–9: "*One of His disciples, Andrew, Simon Peter's brother, said to Him, 'there is a lad here who has five barley loaves and two small fish, but what are they among so many?'*" You know the rest of the story. Jesus took what the boy had in his hands and fed the multitude. After-ward, they collected 12 baskets of leftovers. Knowing the character of Jesus and His disciples, we are safe in assuming that they didn't shake the lad down for his lunch. Rather, it seems the lad offered up what little he had—which was also *all* that he had—and watched God use it in such a way that this feat is the only miracle mentioned in all four of the gospels. Moses and the lad demonstrate that you are neither too old nor too young to do all you can, from wherever you are, with what you've got.

SHINE THE LIGHT

Huge amounts of money are often spent on medical care in the final weeks of one's life. This testifies to the incredible efforts to extend time, if only for hours or days. Time is truly our most valuable asset, because it can never be recovered.

Like all valuable assets, time attracts many robbers. Some robbers, like mindless television, radio, and web surfing, are obvious, while others are often disguised as necessary but are not. This category includes momentary distractions that can evolve into major time drains: unproductive people, low-return tasks and emergencies of the moment that others could handle but look to you to solve. The old poem rings hauntingly true: "Lost, yesterday, somewhere between sunrise and sunset, two golden hours, each set with sixty diamond minutes. No reward is offered for they are gone forever."

One of *THE BOOK*'s strongest warnings concerning time instructs us to redeem the time because the days are evil (see Ephesians 5:16). You redeem time much like you redeem a coupon, by exchanging it for something more valuable. Here are four tradeoffs you can make to begin your time redemption process:

1. **Trade the mindless for the meaningful.** "Mindless" activities include but are not limited to: hours of daily television, playing computer games, web browsing and chatting, and spending more time updating your social media sites like Twitter and Facebook than you do investing in your relationship with God and others who should mean the most to you. Imagine the state of your spiritual, mental, and emotional health if you'd spent the same amount of time deepening your love and knowledge of God and family as you do engaging in the mindless.

2. **Trade what's amusing for what's eternal.** What's amusing can include many of the actions I listed in point one. But we could also add the time you spend studying the lives of celebrities and your favorite sporting teams on web sites, through magazines, and via the

check-out lane's lineup of "trash" publications. What impact could you have on your family, employees, church, and community if you'd redirect the time and energy you invest in what's amusing for pursuits that carry with them eternal value?

3. **Trade improvisation for preparation.** Preparation and the discipline it requires broaden your path to success, because the more you prepare, the less you have to repair. Thus, you have the ability to go deeper and do more with your priorities since you don't have to waste time correcting the missteps or cleaning up messes that result from the improvisation of "winging it," or making your day up as it goes along. The time you invest in structuring your day in advance and building your schedule around the discipline of priorities is an investment that pays hourly dividends as you traverse through your day. Failing to plan may "save" you time up front, but the price you'll pay for living life on such sloppy terms extolls significant losses of momentum, self-esteem, and success throughout the duration of your life.

4. **Trade regret for execution.** People who "web surf" through their days end up living their lives racked with the pain of regret. In fact, it is often the sweat of their deathbed that wakes them to the fact that they missed their life! They were so engaged in the trivial, mindless, and amusing that they didn't invest enough in what really mattered. They improvised their way through life with no real plan or focus and now utter one of the saddest dialogues known to man: "I could have, I should have, if only I would have. . . . "

Instead of practicing the execution of staying in their zone, giving up what matters least for what matters most, pursuing and living God's will for their life, and enthusiastically pursuing the development and application of their God-given talents, they did it "their way" and will one day realize it's too late to get back what they've lost. Don't let this happen to you! Redeem your time! The days are evil, and one of Satan's best tricks is to so seduce you by the distractions around you, that you are unable to focus on God's will for you.

"Sir, we would like to see Jesus" (John 12:20–26). The "Greeks" who wanted to see Jesus may have been Gentiles present to observe the spectacular Jewish festival of Passover or perhaps Greek-speaking Jews. In either case, they had their own agenda in asking to see Jesus. Curiosity.

Christ seemed to ignore the request when it was passed on to Him. Instead He spoke of His coming death. Jesus had an agenda set by the Father, and nothing would distract Him from doing the Father's will. (Don't work off of others' agendas.)

SUMMARY

Human beings develop to their potential in highly structured environments. Whether you're a great athlete, musician, artist, or business person, you cannot expect to reach your potential if you "wing it" every day, operate out of instinct, or make your days up as you go along. But highly structured days must be built around the discipline of right priorities, in which you do first things first, maximize your talents, and stop doing the things that take you out of your zone. Without narrowing your daily focus, you'll engage in the trivial, surrender to every emergency, dabble in areas of personal weakness; likewise, your precious time is likely to come under the control of the most dominant people in your life—because if you don't use your time then someone else will! THE BOOK says that we will be held accountable for every idle word that we speak. The possibility of being held just as accountable for the time that we waste is a mighty incentive to incorporate the four mandates for maximizing your time found in this chapter!

REVELATION

I've shared four mandates to help you maximize your greatest resource each day: your time. The keys to all four are focus and discipline. As Paul wrote in 1 Corinthians 9:26–27: *"Therefore, I run thus; not with uncertainty. Thus, I fight, not as one who beats the air. But I discipline my body and bring it into subjection, lest, when I have preached to others, I myself should become dis-qualified.*" You may believe that you need more time, but the fact is that you're not going to get it! Rather, you must begin to maximize the time you already have. A good use of that time would be answering the five questions in your next Action Exercise.

ACTION EXERCISE

FOUR MANDATES TO MAXIMIZE YOUR TIME!

Answer the following as specifically as possible:

1. Which area for maximizing your time holds the highest potential for you?

   _____

2. List your priorities for the current week:

   _____

   _____

   _____

3. What are your work talents that comprise your "zone"?

   _____

4. How well do your answers for Questions 2 and 3 align?

   _____

5. What must you stop doing in order to spend more time in your "zone"?

   _____

CHAPTER 3

How to Overcome the Number One Cause of Management Failure

GENESIS

The more I study the Bible, and the more I learn about humility, the more I realize how arrogant I've been throughout my life. Starting as a kid, I was aloof, judgmental, and put on airs to make others believe I was something I was not. I followed the example of my parents, who lived above their means and took great strides to keep up with others. I overheard countless conversations where they'd complain that they deserved better and were universally underappreciated. I fell into the pride trap early in life and, decades later, still battle—oftentimes unsuccessfully—to replace my arrogance with the cultivation of humility. And the more I pursue humility, the more I become aware that I need it.

For decades I had the wrong idea about humility. I thought that humble people were wimps, doormats, timid little souls who served as whipping posts for the world's hard-chargers and achievers. As I worked my way up the management ladder, I feigned humility — "Well, I couldn't have done it without the team" — while secretly believing I was the center of the team's universe. I made a point of dressing just a little bit better than everyone else, flashing more bling than my counterparts, and using my verbal prowess as a tool to bring others down rather than edify them. I was prone to conduct "If I were in charge around here things would be different" conversations and complained to my wife how no one truly appreciated the great job I was doing, and that one day they'd realize it when I left the organization and found someone who would understand and acclaim my genius.

I wish that I could say a lot has changed since then, but pride is a persistent problem for me. Pride has cost me plenty: money, old friends, potential new friends, unnecessary debt, prestige, the esteem of colleagues, opportunities, separation from God, self-respect, the ability to impact others, and the list could sadly continue for pages, but I'll cut it short before I talk myself into a depression. As I've become more aware of the devastation pride causes individuals and organizations, I've rounded off some of my most arrogant edges, but a slight air of superiority is always creeping around in my lower nature, just waiting for a weak moment to reveal to the world how far I still have to travel on the lifelong journey to becoming a humble man. It gives me only a modicum of consolation to discover how pride infects so many other men and women from all levels of society as it does me: the rich and poor alike, both the highly accomplished and the lifelong failures, uneducated and academics, young and old, from floor sweepers to CEOs.

I disclose this embarrassing weakness to you because it is dangerous to write a chapter on humility. It may give readers the idea that I've got a handle on my pride and have reached a point where it is no longer a problem. Nothing could be further from the truth; I'm a painstakingly slow work in progress! In this chapter, I share with you my observations concerning pride and humility, biblically promised consequences of both traits, and steps to replace pride with humility. It is my sincere hope that you are a quicker study in the realm of cultivating humility than I have been because being humble brings you peace, growth, attracts others to you, and opens you up to receive God's greater blessings, mercy, and grace in both your business life and your personal life.

Incidentally, there are only five places in the entire BOOK where a "good" or positive pride is mentioned: 2 Corinthians 5:12, 7:4, 8:24; Galatians 6:4; and James 1:9–10. In these cases the words refer to being satisfied with some aspect of your life or another person. They are not used to promote comparison but a humble appreciation and sense of gratitude.

By THE BOOK Blessing

As a sin, pride is unique because whereas other sins separate you from God, pride causes you to attack God. Your independence, selfishness, and self-reliance attempt to dethrone Him and enthrone yourself as your own god.

PRIDE: THE CULPRIT AT THE CORE

I'm going to present a dozen of the most common causes for management failure. This is not a complete list, but it's a pretty good picture of what causes leaders to lose their ability to lead effectively. As you read over this dirty dozen, consider that the ostensible cause listed for each point has, as its core, pride. In other words, when you peel back the onion of what causes leaders to fail, the common denominator at the core and behind them all is pride/arrogance. In fact, many of the listed causes of management failure are also causes of relationship failure! This fact alone greatly raises the stakes of failing to cultivate the humility necessary to put your pride in check and diminish or reduce pride's potential to bring failure to all aspects of your life.

The Dirty Dozen Causes of Management Failure

1. **Failing to build a team and becoming overwhelmed.** Pride causes you to become too dependent upon yourself: never delegating, refusing to empower others, and solving every problem/making all decisions personally until you reach a point of exhaustion and

ineffectiveness. Failing to build a team evinces the arrogance of micromanagement because pride wants to control people, whereas humility wants to serve them.

2. **Perpetual plateau as a result of becoming unteachable.** Pride causes you to become comfortable with your current skill and knowledge level, and turn into a "know-it-all." Your "intelligence arrogance" becomes a disabling ignorance. As a result, you are outgrown by peers and competitors alike.

3. **High turnover within a department.** The number one reason followers leave an organization is to escape a bad manager. One or many of these pride-induced causes for leadership failure will contribute to followers deciding to leave.

4. **Low morale due to lack of positive reinforcement.** Failing to give positive reinforcement to worthy performers can result in high levels of employee apathy and indifference. When your ego prevents you from giving credit when due, you injure morale, break momentum, and cause employees to mentally check out of their jobs.

5. **Distrust from employees because of character issues like failing to admit mistakes.** Once you break trust with employees, you no longer earn commitment; you must settle for compliance. You can break trust through double standards, failing to admit mistakes, not keeping commitments or promises, and a host of other pride-induced character flaws.

6. **Unwillingness to listen to others or involve them in decision-making processes.** When you fail to listen to others, you disengage their hearts and minds and also begin to develop personal blind spots. The only reason you would fail to listen to others is if you don't value others—an attitude rooted in arrogance!

7. **Failing to seek out feedback and make behavioral adjustments.** This arrogant tendency frustrates subordinates and superiors alike. Listening to feedback is a good start but it's not enough. *Seeking it out*, insisting on it if necessary, and then acting upon it overcomes the pride that would cause you to shun the input of others and miss the opportunity to improve all aspects of your performance.

8. **Becoming selfish and territorial.** This attitude creates within you *The Disease of Me*, creating enemies throughout the organization, calling your motives into question, and causing you to lose your influence. *The Disease of Me* offends God by self-exaltation, offends others by self-occupation, and damages you by self-deception.

9. **Putting your own agenda ahead of the team's.** Pride can cause you to commit a cause to yourself, rather than committing yourself to a cause. It promotes leading by personal convenience rather than by personal example. When you put your own comfort ahead of what's best for the team, you break trust with followers. Becoming overly ambitious and shamelessly promoting and pushing yourself ahead of the pack may give the appearance that you are on the fast track for a while. But eventually your corrupt motives cause you to self-destruct, and no one will mourn your demise.

10. **Failing to accept responsibility for your actions and results.** Pride will cause you to live in denial and blame others for your failures. Remain in this state long enough and the problems become insurmountable, because you'll never be able to change what you don't acknowledge.

11. **A variety of character flaws.** Flaws like lying, anger, cheating, stealing, lust, the manipulation of others, and taking shortcuts are evidence of pride because you rationalize compromising the means to achieve the end. Your arrogance convinces you that you are above the disciplines and standards of behavior others must abide by.

12. **Becoming isolated and out of touch.** Pride can cause you to believe you don't need people or that you don't need to spend time with people. Losing touch with the human assets in an organization, substituting rules for relationships, and being perceived as uncaring, preoccupied, or inaccessible puts the bull's-eye of inevitable failure on your back. In time, you will suffer a fast and lonely fall, and the leadership orphans in your organization will sigh with relief at your departure.

By THE BOOK Blessing

Let nothing be done through selfish ambition or conceit, but in lowliness of mind let each esteem others better than himself. Let each of you look out not only for his own interests, but also for the interests of others. (Philippians 2:3–4)

By THE BOOK Leadership Lesson

The Danger of Self-Interest

THE BOOK is filled with stories of leaders who created havoc for others and suffered personally due to their pride-driven self-interest. Many of today's headlines convince us that not much has changed: CEOs of failed companies insist on multimillion-dollar bonuses; congressmen presiding over a trillion-dollar deficit vote themselves thousands of dollars in pay raises; sports stars who demand so much for themselves that team owners are unable to pay other team members what they deserve or attract other key players who could help the team win. Following is just a short list of BOOK-inspired Scriptures and stories that warn against self-interest:

1. Proverbs 27:2: *"Let another man praise you and not your own mouth. A stranger and not your own lips."*
2. Proverbs 14:12: *"There is a way that seems right to a man, but its end is the way of death."*
3. Proverbs 25:27: *"It is not good to eat much honey; so to seek one's own glory is not glory."*
4. Genesis 13 tells how Abram gave his nephew, Lot, the choice of which land he would choose and that Lot selfishly chose the best land for himself even though it was next to the exceedingly evil Sodom and Gomorrah. His self-interest eventually cost him the very property he coveted.
5. The Book of Numbers describes how 10 of the 12 spies Moses sent to evaluate the Promised Land for 40 days returned with frightening reports motivated by their own fear of loss if Israel invaded what God

had promised them. Their negativity stirred up all of Israel with unbelief, causing God to strike the spies dead on the spot and forbid Israel from entering the Promised Land for 40 years: a one-year penalty for each day the spies spent on their mission.

6. Solomon's self-interest caused him to turn his heart from God as he married 700 women and took on 300 concubines! As a result, God tore the kingdom from him and gave it to his servant.

7. Judas, who betrayed Jesus, was the only disciple with an official office—treasurer. Yet he stole money and eventually sold Jesus out for 30 pieces of silver. Soon thereafter, Judas committed suicide.

8. Acts 5 explains how Ananias and his wife, Sapphira, sold property to give money to the newly formed church. However, they conspired to withhold some of the money for themselves, setting a dangerous precedent of self-interest in the newly formed organization. When Peter confronted each one concerning their selfishness and lies, God struck them dead where they stood.

9. Perhaps James, Jesus' half-brother, said it best in his letter to early believers: *"For where envy and self-seeking exist, confusion and every evil thing are there"* (James 3:16).

By THE BOOK Blessing

The most persistent barrier to leading like Jesus is a heart motivated by self-interest, and pride is at the core of self-interest.

TWELVE TERRIBLE TRUTHS ABOUT PRIDE

Now that you can connect most any imaginable management failure directly to pride, let's examine some of the terrible truths about pride. The following facts should create the urgency necessary to begin replacing pride with humility in all aspects of your life.

1. The Scriptures don't have one positive thing to say about pride, nor do they make one positive promise to the proud!

2. The Bible clearly states that God despises pride; opposes the proud; will punish the proud; that pride brings nothing but strife; and more! See Proverbs 3:34, 6:17, 16:18, 13:10, and Malachi 4:1.

3. Pride is satanic in origin. It was a catalyst for Satan's fall as he rallied one-third of the angels to rebel against God, resulting in their eviction from heaven. Thus, pride must be considered satanic as it not only opposes God but attacks Him.

4. There is little that provides greater evidence of pride than prayerlessness. Prayerlessness displays a self-reliance and independence that God finds reprehensible. Consider Psalms 10:4: "*The wicked in his proud countenance does not seek God; God is in none of his thoughts.*" Business leaders have plenty to pray about and for: wisdom, vision, their people, and their customers, for starters. You will never find a humble person who does not pray faithfully, fervently, and frequently.

5. Pride and violence are connected in Scripture. See Psalms 73:6–9. Just as humility and obedience are connected, so are pride and violence.

6. Pride says, "I deserve better," whether referring to a table in a restaurant, your chair placement at a board meeting, or your end-of-the-year bonus. This prideful attitude shows a blatant ignorance of your spiritual condition.

7. Most proud people do not recognize their pride. However, pride is normally the trait they detest most in others. We are irritated when others speak endlessly of themselves, promote themselves, or position themselves, yet don't even realize when we do the same.

8. Pride causes you to trivialize what you do to others and exaggerates what others do to you. The proud often live in deep states of denial and go through life looking for reasons to be offended.

9. Proud people are very critical and don't give honor to anyone, even God. The proud feel obligated to find fault, criticize, and complain as though there were a reward for doing so!

10. Pride becomes very destructive when it causes you to inflate your worth and overlook or justify your sins. This blinds you to your flaws and the subsequent opportunity to improve them.

11. Proud people cannot be trusted because they don't value the commitments they've made to others. They also lose trust from their leaders because they are prone to rebel against those whose charge they are under.

12. Proud people are not grateful for what they have. This is because they assume they're merely getting what they have coming to them. At the same time, what they do get is rarely good enough! Henry Ward Beecher[1] said: "A proud man is seldom a grateful man, for he never thinks he gets as much as he deserves."

By THE BOOK Blessing

One of the most misunderstood adages in business is "never be satisfied." "Never be satisfied" isn't a license for ingratitude. The healthy understanding of "never be satisfied" mandates that you should always be grateful for what you have while you aspire to gain what else it is that you want.

SIX FOLLIES OF PRIDE

If the 12 terrible truths about pride rile you up in resolve to overcome this sin, then perhaps the following six follies of pride will put a boot in your backside to move you along on the road to humility at an even faster clip.

1. **Pride is foolish because of what God has to say about pride and humility.**[2]
   A. Proverbs 3:34: "*Surely he scorns the scornful but gives grace to the humble.*"
   B. Proverbs 13:10: "*By pride comes nothing but strife, but with the well-advised is wisdom.*"
   C. Psalms 18:27: "*For You will save the humble people, but will bring down haughty looks.*"
   D. Proverbs 22:4: "*By humility and the fear of the Lord are riches, honor, and life.*"

2. **Pride is foolish because, apart from Christ, you have nothing to be proud about.**[3] The great evangelist Charles Spurgeon said: "The more thou hast, the more thou art in debt to God; and thou shouldst not be proud of that which renders thee a debtor."[4]

   The Apostle Paul wrote in I Corinthians 4:7: *"For who makes you differ from another? And what do you have that you did not receive? Now if you did indeed receive it, why do you boast as if you have not received it?"*

3. **Pride is foolish because of what pride produces.**[5] As stated in Proverbs, pride produces nothing but strife. Here are four examples:

   A. **Pride is foolish because it causes you to forget about God.**[6] Consider John's words when he wrote to relay Christ's message to the rich but complacent Laodicean church: *"I know your works, that you are neither cold nor hot. So then, because you are lukewarm, and neither cold nor hot, I will vomit you out of my mouth. Because you say, 'I am rich, have become wealthy, and have need of nothing'—and do not know you are wretched, miserable, poor blind and naked"* (Revelation 3:15–17).

   B. **Pride is foolish because it causes you to make poor decisions.**[7] Read the following progression of passages to see how, in seven short verses, King Jehosophat facilitated his own rapid decline by forgetting about God and making poor decisions: 2 Chronicles 20:30: *"Then the realm of Jehosophat was quiet, for his God gave him rest all around"* . . . 35: *"After this Jehosophat king of Judah allied himself with Ahaziah king of Israel, who acted very wickedly"* . . . 37: *"Because you have allied yourself with Ahaziah, the Lord has destroyed your works."*

   C. **Pride is foolish because it causes you to act wickedly.**[8] Read the following passage concerning Uzziah to see just how fast God can bring consequences to you when you stop seeking Him and begin to act wickedly out of your own sense of strength and worth. Notice that his demise begins with the transition from the days he sought the Lord to becoming strong with his heart lifted up (prideful):

2 Chronicles 26:5: *He (Uzziah) sought God in the days of Zech-ariah, who had understanding in the vision of God; and as long as he sought the Lord, God made him prosper . . .* 16: *But when he was strong his heart was lifted up, to his destruction, for he transgressed against the Lord his God by entering the temple of the Lord to burn incense on the altar of incense . . .* 19: *And while he was angry with the priests, leprosy broke out on his forehead, before the priests in the house of the Lord, beside the incense altar.*

D. **Pride is foolish because it causes you to sin with your speech.**[9] You tend to gossip, criticize, lie, become profane, and plant seeds of discord when you lose your focus on God and put it on yourself. In fact, without a deliberate, Spirit-filled endeavor to cultivate humility, you'll never tame your tongue. This is why James wrote: *"But no man can tame the tongue. It is an unruly evil, full of deadly poison"* (James 3:8).

4. **Pride is foolish because of the biblical consequences of pride.**[10] God will oppose you. Pride comes before destruction. The proud will be burned up as stubble. Wow! You probably have enough challenges in your business each day without riling up this sort of wrath!

Herod Had Worms

Herod and Nebuchadnezzar provide vivid reminders of the con-sequences pride brings to leaders who forget about God!

Acts 12:21–23: *"So on a set day Herod, arrayed in royal apparel, sat on his throne and gave an oration to them. And the people kept shouting, 'The voice of a god and not of a man!' Then, immediately, an angel of the Lord struck him because he did not give glory to God. And he was eaten by worms and died."*

The Herod referred to in this instance was Herod Agrippa I, the grandson of Herod the Great, whom the wise men visited, and who ordered the slaughter of the innocent children in an attempt to kill Jesus. He is the nephew of Herod Antipas, who had John the Baptist killed and presided over the trial of Jesus. Herod Agrippa I had the apostle James, the brother of John, murdered and planned on doing the same to Peter. He lay sick and dying for five days after being stricken by God for his pride and was eaten from the inside out by a type of tapeworm. This was in A.D. 44.

Nebuchadnezzar: Trouble with "I" and "My"!

Going back a few centuries to around 582 B.C., learn a lesson in vocabulary from the life of a king.

> The king (Nebuchadnezzar) spoke, saying, 'Is not this great Babylon, that I have built for a royal dwelling by my mighty power and for the honor of my majesty?' While the words were still in the King's mouth, a voice fell from heaven: 'King Nebuchadnezzar, to you it is spoken: The kingdom has departed from you! And they shall drive you from men, and your dwelling shall be with the beasts of the field. They shall make you eat grass like oxen; and seven times shall pass over you, until you come to know the Most High rules in the kingdom of men, and gives it to whomever He chooses.' (Daniel 4:30)

To the many benefits of cultivating humility for your personal and business life, you can now add the less likely chances of your being eaten alive by worms or spending seven years insanely crawling around on all fours eating grass like an ox!

To continue with the six follies of pride:

5. **Pride is foolish because it is a trait of evil and not righteousness.**[11]
   Pride clearly reveals your heart condition and the bankruptcy of your spiritual life.
6. **Pride is foolish because Christ was humble and you must conform to His image.**[12]
   A. Connect Romans 8:29 with Mark 10:45 and you'll gain a clear picture that as leaders we are to imitate Christ and His humility.

B. *"For whom He foreknew, He also predestined to be conformed to the image of His Son, that He might be the firstborn of many brethren"* (Romans 8:29).

C. *"For even the Son of Man did not come to be served, but to serve and to give His life a ransom for many"* (Mark 10:45).

By THE BOOK Blessing

To truly understand what it means to forsake pride and live humbly, you must study the life of Christ. In the one and only biblical passage where Jesus describes his own character traits, He says:

> Come to Me, all you who labor and are heavy laden, and I will give you rest. Take My yoke upon you and learn from Me, for I am gentle and lowly in heart *and you will find rest for your souls.* (author's emphasis) (Matthew 11:28–29)

Rx for Pride: Humility

After discussing the 12 causes of management failure all rooted in pride, the 12 terrible truths about pride, and the six follies of pride, it's time to focus on pride's Rx: humility. What makes humility difficult is that it doesn't come naturally; pride does! Thus, humility must be cultivated. And it is a lifelong journey. In fact, just about the time you begin to think you're humble, you're not!

Eight Ways to Cultivate Humility

1. **Know that you are not superior to anyone else.**[13] The next time you're ready to judge someone or feel superior to them in some way, embrace the attitude of the publican from Luke 8:13: *"Lord, have mercy on me, a sinner."* Reciting this verse has a supernatural ability to humble you before God and men.

   You can also judge how big a person you are by how well you treat "little" people: the receptionist, the waiter, the kid selling cookies at your doorstep, the entry-level employee, the house-keeper, and the like. The words of Charles Spurgeon ring true in this regard: "Humility is to make a right estimate of one's self."[14]

Here is a wake-up call for you, Mr. or Ms. "Potentially Arrogant" CEO: If Jesus Christ can get down on his knees and wash the two dozen stinking feet of His followers, you can also regard your people in a manner that says, "I need you more than you need me."

2. **Do not be obnoxious in appearance or behavior.**[15] The three things you should most heavily depend upon to bring you attention in the workplace are not your clothes, jewelry, or hairstyle but your character, competence, and consistency. In fact, those who lack these qualities often resort to other attention-getting diversions to shift attention away from their defective performance and onto some other aspect of their life.

   Ultimately, at work and at home, live to bring attention and glory to God, not to yourself. According to Isaiah 48:11, God is not interested in giving or sharing His glory with you: *"And I will not give my glory to another."* Heed the words of Thomas Watson: "The proud man is the mark which God shoots at. And He never misses His mark."

3. **Do not be assuming.**[16] Proverbs 26:6–7 warns: *"Do not exalt yourself in the presence of the king, and do not stand in the place of the great. For it is better that he say to you, 'Come up here,' than you should be put lower in the presence of the prince . . ."*

   Being assuming can also mean that you wait for someone else to make the first move: to apologize, to introduce himself to you, to pick up the check at lunch, to volunteer to do more than their share, to make the sacrifice, and so on. Follow the advice of James: *"Humble yourselves in the sight of the Lord, and He will lift you up"* (4:10).

4. **Do not be scornful or contentious.**[17] Scornful people look for trouble. They go through the workplace with a chip on their shoulders the size of a lumber yard. They're spoiling for a fight. Eventually, they self-destruct. It's important to keep the double promise of Proverbs 3:34 in mind: *"Surely He scorns the scornful but*

gives grace to the humble." These two promises are so potent that James and Peter both quoted this passage in their letters.

Numbers 12 gives a telling illustration of God's promise to scorn the scornful and give grace to the humble as Moses' own sister and brother became jealous of his leadership: *"Then Miriam and Aaron spoke against Moses because of the Ethiopian woman whom he had married. . . . So they said, 'Has the Lord indeed spoken only through Moses? Has He not spoken through us also?' And the Lord heard it."* (Now the man Moses was very humble, more than all men who were on the face of the earth.) (Numbers 12:1–3).

To make a long story short, the Lord came down in the pillar of cloud and personally took Aaron and Miriam to task for speaking against his humble servant Moses, chastising them and striking Miriam with a temporary case of leprosy. Scorn to the scornful and grace to the humble indeed!

5. **Don't always insist on having your way.**[18] Humble people are inflexible in nothing except their values. Being stubborn and willful by insisting on having your way is a surefire sign of pride. Maintaining flexibility and giving others a chance to make decisions, employ their ideas, solve their own problems, and have their way, builds a wall of humility around you that will be difficult for pride to penetrate. In the words of Jonathan Edwards: "Nothing sets a person so much out of the devil's reach as humility."[19]

6. **Submit to authority.**[20] Yes, this means your boss, even if you don't care for him or her, and your government, even if you didn't vote for who is in office. Consider that even though he tried to kill David, David mourned the death of Saul and put to death the man who had killed God's anointed (2 Samuel 1:1–15). Christ paid taxes to human authorities: to the same government He knew would murder Him. And Paul wrote, *"Render therefore to all their due: taxes to whom taxes are due, customs to whom customs, fear to whom fear, honor to whom honor"* (Romans 13:7).

Just as leaders are expected to be humble, so are followers! Respect the hard work of your leaders, give them your support, follow their direction, help them carry their load, and don't try to change them or second-guess them. However, when your leader asks you to do something that violates the laws of God, you should remember to fear God more than man, but handle the issue as prescribed by Paul in his letter to Timothy:

> And the Lord's servant must not quarrel; instead he must be kind to everyone, able to teach, not resentful. Those who oppose him he must gently instruct, in the hope that God will grant them repentance leading them to a knowledge of the truth, and that they will come to their senses and escape from the trap of the devil, who has taken them captive to do his will. (2 Timothy 2:24–26)

If those in authority insist that you violate the laws of God, then you should be encouraged by the words of Paul to the Galatians and leave the organization: *"For do I now persuade men, or God? Or do I seek to please men? For if I still pleased men, I would not be a bondservant of Christ"* (Galatians 1:10).

7. **Seek out and be open to Biblical instruction, reproof, rebuke, and constructive criticism.**[21] Use your critics to fine-tune your leadership style and ability in all areas of your life, and employ their complaints or constructive criticism to improve all aspects of your organization. Just as the 80,000 hewers sanded the stones so that they would fit perfectly as the workers built Solomon's Temple, let your own "hewers" smooth your rough edges and perfect you to become a better leader in all aspects of your life.

Following are four Scriptures that will help you embrace this discipline:

A. *"As many as I love, I rebuke and chasten. Therefore be zealous and repent"* (Revelation 3:19).

B. *"Whoever loves instruction loves knowledge, but he who hates correction is stupid"* (Proverbs 12:1).

    C. *"Poverty and shame will come to him who disdains correction, but he who regards a rebuke will be honored"* (Proverbs 13:18).

    D. *"Now no chastening seems to be joyful for the present, but painful; nevertheless, afterward it yields the peaceable fruit of righteousness to those who have been trained by it"* (Hebrews 12:11).

8. **Learn to receive.** Cultivating humility is more than giving; it is setting your pride aside so that you may also receive. Many Christians are eager to do for others but have a difficult time letting someone return the favor, never realizing that their failure to receive is rooted in pride. Learning to receive covers a lot of ground: allowing someone to help you with a task, asking for help with your work, asking for directions, letting someone else pick up the dinner check, and being okay with a friend buying you a Christmas present without feeling obligated to reciprocate.

In the thirteenth chapter of John, as He is washing the disciple's feet, Jesus gives Peter a lesson in how to receive:

> Then He came to Simon Peter. And Peter said to Him, "Lord, are You washing my feet?"
>
> Jesus answered him, "What I am doing you do not understand now, but you will know after this."
>
> Peter said to Him, "You shall never wash my feet!"
>
> Jesus answered him, "If I do not wash you; you have no part with Me."
>
> Simon Peter said to Him, "Lord, not my feet only, but also my hands and my head!" (John 13:6–9)

Rhonda, my wife, is a giver. Consequently, it's always been tough for her to ask for or receive help because she goes to great pains to not inconvenience anyone. One thing that has helped her get better at receiving over the years is the understanding that by not letting others do for her, she robs them of the blessing that comes from giving.

By THE BOOK Blessing

Here's a prayer worth memorizing and repeating every day. It was written by the renowned Scottish evangelist Andrew Murray, who happened to write a very good book on the subject of humility:

"Dear God, out of Your great goodness, make known to me and take away every form of pride, whether it is from evil spirits or my own corrupt nature; and that You will awaken in me the deepest depth and truth of that humility which can make me capable of Your light and Holy Spirit."

By THE BOOK LESSON IN LEADERSHIP

DANGER AT THE TOP OF THE MOUNTAIN!

After years of consulting with business leaders, I have discovered that they are most prone to do something foolish right at the conclusion of a great victory. Something about getting to the top of the mountain can make you feel bullet-proof, self-reliant, and proud. As a result of success, it's easier to let up on accountability, training, recruiting, taking care of customers, making needed changes and decisions, and taking mature risks. You stop listening to others, start counting more on your own wisdom, and forget about God until your foolishness causes you to fall and cry out to Him again!

THE BOOK is filled with examples of leaders who blew it once they reached the pinnacle of success—as they were standing at the top of the mountain, at the peak of their game, in the wake of a major accomplishment. World and business histories show that at the crescendo of success many leaders let their guard down and abandon the very character and discipline that helped them reach that point in the first place. The three following examples harbor strong warnings for successful leaders who want to sustain and increase their success and not ride a roller coaster of inconsistency brought upon by pride or arrogance.

Samson: Samson was the strongest man in the world. He was given his gift to help free his people from the Philistines, but he selfishly used

72

his strength to pursue his own ends. One of Samson's great victories came when he killed a thousand of the enemy with the jawbone of a donkey. After his victory, he was thirsty and God accommodated him by miraculously splitting the hollow in Lehi from which water gushed forth. At the top of his game and basking in the glow of victory, Samson went to Gaza, forgot about God, and slept with a prostitute. Samson's major weakness was lust. Many leaders today are in the same boat and seem to stray the farthest at precisely the point when they have the most to lose. (See Judges 15:14–16:1.)

Jehosophat: Against all odds and with the help of his Maker, King Jehosophat had just won a decisive and unexpected victory over a much more powerful enemy. As a result, his realm was quiet and peaceful. He was at the top of his game. He had conquered his foes. Life was good! But before long, Jehosophat forgot about God and trusted his own wisdom. He decided to ally himself with the wicked King Ahaziah and pick a fight with Tarshish. As a result of his unwise association with the corrupt, his works were destroyed. (See 2 Chronicles 20:2–37.)

Saul: Saul was the first king of Israel and he had just been handed a guaranteed victory over the Amalekites. All he had to do in return was follow God's order to destroy them and all that they had, so that they would never again hinder God's chosen people. Saul, in his own wisdom, decided that after the battle was won, he wouldn't destroy *everything* but would instead keep plenty of "good" livestock for himself and let the conquered king live. This rebellion and arrogance while at the top of the mountain planted the seeds for his rejection as king of Israel. (See 1 Samuel 15:1–26.)

It's been suggested that leaders need more spiritual help and guidance when they're at the top of the mountain than when they're in dire straits. Perhaps this is why Jesus, after feeding the five thousand, immediately retreated to a mountain for prayer (Mark 6:46). This begs the question: In the wake of a great victory where do you head, to the bar or to your knees?

Mountaintop experiences can be incredible! But they are also the point where unaware leaders become prideful, impulsive, and corrupt, simultaneously planting the seeds to their eventual decline. Be aware of this pitfall, and resolve to do better so that you can be a leader who will last over the long haul.

SHINE THE LIGHT

I believe that most people fail to understand that their lack of peace and joy in any area of life is rooted in their pride. Let's shine the light on why this is:

1. You can only have true peace and joy when you totally surrender your life to God and subordinate your will to His. Without a doubt, you must give up control in order to go up in peace and joy.

2. Pride prevents this total surrender. Many contend that they have faith, and thus, they do live their lives in submission to God. But you can have faith and still fail to completely surrender all areas of your life, pridefully clinging to control over aspects such as finances, your workplace behavior, the television and movies you watch, investments, partnerships, prejudices, the language that you use, and more. Some Christians excuse excluding God from various areas of their life with the defense, "Some day I will turn this over to God. But I need to clean up some things and work through a few issues first." This strategy serves only to extend pride's assault on your life, because delayed obedience is disobedience, and disobedience always carries consequences.

3. The parts of your life that you fail to surrender to God are the precise sectors where you will lack the most peace and joy. You can count on this, because a lack of surrender indicates deficient trust, and insufficient trust leads to disobedience to God's word and ways. As a result of your pride-induced distrust and disobedience, you decide to do it "your way" and will suffer the consequences that come when you depart from God and rely on your own strength, experience, and wisdom. These consequences include but are not

limited to the following: stress, worry, poor decision making, wasted resources, frustration, hopelessness, failure, and depression. These consequences reaffirm the wisdom of Proverbs 13:10: *"By pride comes nothing but strife."*

Shine the light on your own life for a moment. Where do you suffer persistent stress and most consistently lack peace and joy? Could it be because your pride has hardened your heart, causing you to demote God to a subordinate role in these areas? If you're at least considering this possibility, it indicates that your pride hasn't totally blinded you to reality or caused you to sink into a dangerous state of spiritual denial. If pride is causing you to stop short of total surrender to God, then renouncing control and giving up these pockets of resistance to Him is your highest priority and should be your next move.

SUMMARY

Sadly, human nature reveals that many who read this chapter will act more humble but remain secretly and ferociously proud. They'll say all the right things—"Oh, it was really nothing" or "Anyone could have done it"—and of course their eyes will cast down, shoulders slumped, hands folded in front of them, blushing on the outside but bluffing from within. Privately, they congratulate themselves and gloat that they are better than the next guy and at least a little bit smarter as well.

How about you? Are you humble for reputation or for real? Are you really willing to give credit away, or do you spin things just a bit to get a tad more than your share? And how about your motives? Little reveals a person's humility or lack of it more than their reason for *why* they did something. Did you do what you did primarily to help the team or to promote yourself? Would it have mattered to you if no one noticed your extra effort as long as you knew in your heart that you gave it your all? Did you work as unto God or as unto men?

There is no greater motivation to slay your pride and cultivate humility than fully understanding what God has to say about both subjects, as outlined in detail in this chapter. He hates pride and opposes the proud while He gives grace to the humble, along with honor, riches, and life. As author C.J. Mahaney has written, "Contrary to the popular and false belief, it is not those who 'help themselves' whom God helps but those who *humble* themselves."[22]

REVELATION

In this chapter I've shown that many causes of the management failures often attributed to other causes are firmly rooted in pride. I expressed in God's own words how He feels about pride. I suppose I could have made my point just as well and saved a lot of space by simply directing you to Proverbs 6 where six things that God hates are itemized, with pride sitting atop the list.

Without question, so much of our success, at work and away from work, depends upon the cultivation of humility. In fact, all nine of the fruits of the Spirit as listed in the fifth chapter of Galatians have humility at their root.

However, many people in the workplace today are afraid of humility. They believe it will make them timid and perceived as weak, a pushover, or a whipping post. On the contrary, humility requires and demonstrates great strength. Take a survey and ask others for the names of the world's most renowned humble leaders and Mother Teresa, Gandhi, and Jesus will show up most every time. But these leaders were far from being timid, weak, or pushovers! Their strength and leadership ability was anchored in their lack of self-interest, their focus on the edification of others, and a willingness to decrease themselves so that others might increase. They all followed—Gandhi without even realizing it—the prescription for great leadership for effective leaders as presented in Micah 6:8: *"He has shown you, O man, what is good, And what does the Lord require of you but to do justly, to love mercy and to walk humbly with your God."* In addition to these words being a prescription, they should be the centerpiece of an effective leader's job description.

ACTION EXERCISE

HOW TO OVERCOME THE NUMBER ONE CAUSE OF MANAGEMENT FAILURE

1. Review the 12 causes of management failure at the beginning of this chapter and determine the following:
   - Which of the 12 most hinder your own performance? Which of the eight steps given to cultivate humility can you most readily apply?
   - List at least three things that your pride has cost you in your personal life. How will you demonstrate more humility in these areas?
2. Which of the 12 causes for management failure most affect your top leader(s)?
   - How will you coach them to overcome this flaw(s)?
3. What suggestions can you offer that will improve this chapter as I teach it in workshops or rewrite it in the future? Write to me directly at dave@learntolead.com.

Five Steps to Build a Rock Solid Character

Genesis

Character is defined by the *Oxford Dictionary* as "the collective qualities or characteristics, especially mental and moral, that distinguish a person or thing; a moral strength, a reputation." Because leaders have the privilege of affecting more people than followers do, the upside value of leaders having rock solid character is difficult to quantify, and the penalty for exhibiting weak character is impossible to calculate. Many character flaws are rooted in the pride issues discussed in the previous chapter. Proud people can become deluded and believe that they are above the rules or the law. Other character infractions are the result of carelessness, taking shortcuts, and the desire for instant gratification.

As a society, we've become accustomed to watching talented and successful people self-destruct because of character issues. Ultimately, they make poor choices, and choices are a big part of what makes up the mental and moral issues that forge our character and distinguish us as human beings. For an example of how ubiquitous character-induced falls from grace are, consider the following news stories that appeared in just a seven-day period as I wrote this chapter: two nominees for cabinet positions in the United States government were discovered to have failed to pay hundreds of thousands of dollars in income taxes; a third candidate for a cabinet position was unable to pay nearly six million dollars in campaign debt; a world champion Olympian and national hero was photographed smoking marijuana; a major league baseball player admitted to stealing memorabilia from his former stadium; and a slew of CEOs continued to defend seven- and eight-figure bonuses from companies they ran into the ground. Although our personal issues may not make the evening news, each of us is susceptible to the same type of poor judgment and decline in our own lives if we don't continually work at building a character that produces right values and elicits correct choices.

As I examine my own career and personal life, I realize that during the times when my world wasn't "right," it was because I wasn't right. And don't be naïve; just because you attend church, or read the Bible, or pray each day doesn't mean that you're "right." There's a significant gap between knowing what is right, and actually doing it! Until you close that gap, you'll continue to fall short of building the character that makes you a leader who is both effective today and will last over the long haul.

In this chapter, I cover five common areas in which business leaders fall short on character issues. There are dozens more that I could add to this list, but I chose these five because they're taken too casually by many leaders or are not even considered to be true character flaws at all when compared with treachery like stealing, substance abuse, and adultery. You'll find that some of the decisions I urge you to make concerning these five character choices go against conventional wisdom in the bare-knuckle world of business competition. However, understanding what THE BOOK has to say about these "lesser" matters should encourage you to improve your outlook concerning them and coach your team to do likewise.

Don't Tell "White Lies"

Are Your Pants on Fire?

Have you ever instructed your receptionist to tell a caller that you weren't in the office, even though you were? If so, then you're a liar. Now, don't get defensive! You'll likely claim that such an insignificant falsehood falls under the *Oxford Dictionary* definition of a white lie, which is to "tell a harmless or trivial untruth." However, I challenge you to find anywhere in THE BOOK where a lie of any sort is sanctioned by God as harmless or trivial. Like so many sins, if you begin to explain away a "lesser" form of it through rationalization, soon you can begin to justify graduated infractions that lead you to major lapses in judgment, bringing devastating consequences that ruin your life. For instance, men have written off as "harmless" the practice of "just looking" as they lustily stare down an attractive woman. "Ain't no crime in looking," they say with a laugh. But a "harmless" leer can lead to "harmless" small talk, which leads to buying one "harmless" drink, which elicits a "harmless" good-night kiss, which brings the desire for "harmless"—and secret— follow-up phone calls, which concludes in a rendezvous that costs you and your family all that you hold dear and thought was sacred.

If you're going to start classifying lies as "white" or "whoppers," you may as well go ahead and categorize different levels of adultery too. What would be an adulterous equivalent of a white lie? Maybe a gentle squeeze or swat on the behind? Or how about a parting hug that is two degrees tighter and three seconds longer than is appropriate? While you're at it, you could justify stealing from the company as well. The white lie version of embezzlement could be taking a few dollars worth of office supplies home with you, or mailing personal correspondence with company postage, or making personal copies on the company Xerox machine. Face the facts. According to THE BOOK, if you tell a lie of any kind, you are a liar; because Satan is referred to as the "father of lies," a liar's label isn't something you should want as part of your reputation.

By THE BOOK Blessing

Therefore, putting away all lying, let each one of you speak truth with his neighbor, for we are members of one another. (Ephesians 5:25)

BY THE BOOK LEADERSHIP LESSON

DAVID'S LIE KILLS 85!

In 1 Samuel 21 through chapter 22:9, you'll read about the drastic consequences resulting from David's white lie to the priest Ahimelech. David was on the run from King Saul and was hungry. He told the priest that he was on the king's business (a "white" lie) and asked for five loaves of bread. The priest accommodated his request and also gave him Goliath's old sword, whereupon David fled in his quest to avoid the pursuing Saul. When Saul found out that Ahimelech had helped David, he ordered the death of the priests whom he accused of conspiring against him and helping David. As a result of David's "trivial and harmless" lie, 85 priests were murdered. David later admitted to Ahimelech's son, "*I have caused the death of all the persons of your father's house*" (I Samuel 22:22). You could certainly argue that a tiny lie like "I'm here on the king's business" should not have led to such drastic consequences. But it did. And that's precisely why *all* lies are serious: you have no way of knowing what it will lead to, how it will impact others, or what it might cost now or in the future.

FOUR WORDS TO WATCH OUT FOR!

Examine areas where you have in the past or may now be telling white lies without even thinking about it or realizing what you're doing. It will help you to know that there are four words that should tip you off that you're headed for trouble: "Just tell them that . . ." "Just tell him that I'm not in." "Just tell her that we no longer have that one in stock." "Just tell him that the offer has already expired." "Just tell them that this is the last one available at that price." "Just tell him that we're not hiring right now." "Just tell her that she doesn't qualify for the special interest rate." "Just tell him that I'm not feeling well." "Just tell him that . . ." normally means you're getting ready to lie. And if someone tells you to say to someone else "Just tell him that . . . ," you can do the person a great service by respectfully replying, "But that's not true, what should I tell him instead?"

To build a rock solid character, do the following:

1. Tell the truth, even when it is not easy, cheap, popular, or convenient.
2. Tell the truth because it is right; because it pleases God; because it protects your personal integrity; and because it honors, rather than diminishes, everyone who hears what you say.
3. Never, ever ask people to sin for you by instructing them to lie on your behalf. This is an abuse of your power, position, relationship, and friendship, and can destroy your witness as a Christian.

By THE BOOK Blessing

He who is faithful in what is least is faithful also in much; and he who is unjust in what is least is unjust also in much. (Luke 16:10)

KEEP YOUR COMMITMENTS

SWEAR TO YOUR OWN HURT

Many leaders make casual promises. Some they never intend to keep: "I'll call you later and we'll talk about it." "If you keep doing a good job, we'll take a hard look at you when the next management slot opens up." Other commitments they intend to fulfill but go back on their word when the price gets too high. They have no trouble justifying their failure to follow through as they explain that "things have changed." I'm speaking from experience in this regard, and there is one particular incident where I didn't fulfill my commitment that continues to cause me regret.

I had volunteered to teach a leadership course in Moscow, twice per year, for three years. There were hundreds of leaders who came to the first five of six seminars I had agreed to conduct. However, the leadership team in Moscow that hosted me had been skimming money from the organization that put on the events, as well as from me personally as they double-billed the sponsor and me for like expenses. We had confronted them over these issues twice and they pleaded ignorance, promising to put stricter measures in place to ensure it didn't happen again. When it *did* happen again during my fifth journey to Russia, I decided that I'd had enough and that I would not return. I was indignant at being cheated, used every logical argument for not returning, and convinced myself that not completing my sixth seminar would serve as a lesson that might encourage more ethical behavior in the future. The problem with my decision was that regardless of how I spun it, the bottom line was that I was failing to do what I had agreed to do three years prior. I should have kept my word, even though it became unpleasant or costly. At least that's what THE BOOK says in Psalms 15:4: "*He who swears to his own hurt and does not change . . . will never be moved.*"

Swearing to your own hurt means that you'll do what you said you'd do, when you said you'd do it, and how you said you'd do it, even if it becomes more costly, inconvenient, or time-consuming than you estimated. In retrospect, I should have returned to Moscow, conducted my final conference, dismissed the corrupt board, and then announced that no one from the organization I represented would ever return to work in their city again until there were ethical leaders in place.

By THE BOOK Blessing

Whoever falsely boasts of giving is like clouds and wind without rain. (Proverbs 25:14)

> ## By THE BOOK Leadership Lesson
> ### Remember to Do What Joshua Didn't!
>
> The ninth chapter of Joshua tells how the Gibeonites tricked Joshua into two things: not destroying their city and defending them against enemies! When Joshua found out he had been duped, he didn't use their deceit as an excuse to break his word. Rather, he swore to his own hurt and did what he said, regardless of the cost. Why? Because he said he would, and his word didn't have small print that disclaimed "as long as it's cheap or easy." However, Joshua 9:14 offers a lesson that you can apply before making a commitment of any consequence: ". . . *but they did not seek the counsel of the Lord.*" Praying for wisdom before you make a vow, rather than trusting your own gut, is a sound strategy for not getting yourself into situations that you beg God to release you from later.

Joshua 10:5–10 tells the story of how the five Amorite kings decided to attack Gibeon in retaliation for its making peace with Joshua and Israel. The panicked Gibeonites sent emissaries to Joshua asking him to honor his word and come to protect them. At this point, Joshua could have told them, "You cheated and deceived me into protecting you. Thus the promise I made you is void!" However, true to his promise, Joshua gathered his men and led them on an all-night march to defend the Gibeonites. Joshua and all of Israel were greatly rewarded for keeping their commitment, as they found the armies of all the Amorites out in the open and vulnerable to the slaughter that they inflicted upon them. Thus, even though Joshua had made a mistake by not seeking God before he agreed to defend the Gibeonites, by keeping his commitment he was rewarded by God with the opportunity to overwhelm his enemy all at once while they were in the open rather than incur the more costly and time-consuming process of invading the five well-fortified Amorite city-states individually.

Cutting Expenses or Breaking a Promise?

In tough economic times, business leaders may be tempted to compromise their character in order to save a buck or two. They begin to back out of agreements they signed their name to—a name that was accepted and assumed as honorable by the other party. Under the guise of "cutting back," they renege on promises to customers, vendors, and employees. If in the good times your mouth wrote checks that your bank account can no longer cash, carefully weigh both the legal and moral cost of breaking your word. Cutting expenses is necessary and understandable, but breaking promises is not. It cheapens and diminishes you both as an organization and as a human being. Anyone failing to fulfill an agreement he or she signed becomes a certifiable liar and a probable cheat.

To build a rock solid character, do the following:

1. Count the cost. Before you commit to anything, make certain that you can live with the worst case scenario resulting from what you're saying "yes" to. Understand that there are no "little" commitments to the person you're committing to!
2. Seek God's wisdom before deciding. Check with trusted counselors who have nothing to gain or lose, either way, from your decision.
3. Follow through. Do what you said you'd do, regardless of the cost—and don't let those last four words cause you to compromise your character!

By THE BOOK Blessing

For which of you, intending to build a tower, does not sit down first and count the cost, whether he has enough to finish it—lest he has laid the foundation, and is not able to finish, all who see it begin to mock him, saying, "This man began to build and was not able to finish." (Luke 14:27–29)

Go the Second Mile

From "Just Enough" to "And Then Some"

Most people wouldn't regard doing only what you are required to do as a character flaw but THE BOOK instructs otherwise. Sadly, an overwhelming number of managers I've asked over the years affirm that, in their experience, a majority of their employees fall under the category of "just enough" workers. They do just enough to get by; just enough to get paid; just enough not to get fired. This puts a premium value on leaders and subordinates alike who have an "and then some" mindset. They do what is required, and then some; hit their goals, and then some; deliver what they promised, and then some. Which best describes your own work ethic: "just enough" or "and then some"? If it's "just enough," my guess is that those who follow you emulate your half-hearted effort. On the other hand, if you're a second-miler, you probably have attracted, inspired, and are retaining the same, because the speed of the leader is the speed of the pack.

I am blessed with an abundance of friends in business with net worths ranging into the billions of dollars. Most of these men and women will readily admit that they are no smarter than their less successful counterparts. They simply outwork them, outthink them, and as a result outperform them. They found that by doing what others were unwilling to do, going where they were unwilling to go, saying what they were unwilling to say, learning what they were unwilling to learn, and risking what they were unwilling to risk, provided a success and lifestyle that the "just enough" crowd is unable to attain. To quote author and motivator Zig Ziglar, "There is no traffic jam on the second mile." This is true because the majority of folks have trouble limping through the first mile, much less bothering themselves with the exertion that would come from going farther.

By THE BOOK Blessing

Whatever your hand finds to do, do it with your might; for there is no work or device or knowledge or wisdom in the grave where you are going. (Ecclesiastes 9:10)

By THE BOOK LESSON IN LEADERSHIP

JESUS DECLARED THAT ENOUGH IS *NOT* ENOUGH!

For Christians who believe that merely doing what you're being paid to do is enough, you'll find a call to the second mile in Luke 17:7–10: "*And which of you, having a servant plowing or tending sheep, will say to him when he has come in from the field, 'Come at once and sit down to eat?' But will he not rather say to him, 'Prepare something for my supper, and gird yourself and serve me 'til I have eaten and drunk, and afterward you will eat and drink?' Does he thank that servant because he did the things that were commanded him? I think not. So likewise you, when you have done all those things which you are commanded, say, 'We are unprofitable servants. We have done what was our duty to do.'*" Did you catch that? According to Christ, if you do only what you are required to do, your performance is nothing special and is unworthy of acclaim. This standard by which your behavior is to be judged takes away going the second mile as an option and makes it mandatory for any leader wanting to lead according to Christ's loftier prescription.

By THE BOOK Blessing

Going the first mile fulfills an obligation. By going the second mile you earn the right to witness and influence.

WHAT A DIFFERENCE A MILE MAKES!

There was open animosity between the Roman authorities and their Jewish subjects. Laws that required a Jew to carry the heavy pack for a Roman soldier one mile only made matters worse. So you can imagine the astonishment at Jesus' teaching that they were to go the second mile! During the first mile, there would probably be very little conversation between the Roman and the Jew. In fact, the soldier would most likely regard the burden bearer as a mere servant and suspect him of inward grumbling because the task he performed fulfilled a legal obligation. Imagine the Roman soldier's total surprise when, at the end of one mile, the servant would say, "I want to carry your pack a second mile." No longer would the Jew be viewed merely as a servant but as a friend. The conversation would have a whole new basis for significance and would no doubt begin with this question: "Why are you doing this?" The Jewish man would then be able to explain the teaching he learned from Jesus, and because this teaching had changed his life, the soldier would be open to hearing more. The second mile would earn the Jew a hearing that would open the door for him to influence authorities. The same is true for you, regardless of your position in your organization. You can give a thousand speeches on hard work and dedication, but your speeches will never match the impact you can make when you really walk that second mile, because people will be able to go from listening to your sermon to watching it.

To build a rock solid character, do the following:

1. Accept the concept that each day you do less than you can, you become less than you are—personally, and in the eyes of others.
2. Embrace the promise of Galatians 6:9: *"And let us not grow weary while doing good, for in due season we shall reap if we do not lose heart."*
3. Realize that you may be one phone call away, one skill away, one discipline away, or one effort away from your next breakthrough. Make your goal to be totally used up when you die, leaving this earth with no regrets—no "I should haves," no "I could haves," and no "If only I would haves."

By THE BOOK Blessing

And whatever you do, do it heartily, as to the Lord and not to men, knowing that from the Lord you will receive the reward of the inheritance; for you serve the Lord Christ. (Colossians 3:23)

Don't Give False Impressions

Giving false impressions in business covers a lot of ground: advertising to lead someone to believe they'll get something they won't; spinning the reality of your contribution to a task to gain undeserved credit; covering up the reality of your fault for a problem to escape warranted punishment; misleading a job candidate to think that the position, pay, or company is more than it really is; offering excuses to disguise reality; using flowery language to hide the truth; omitting facts that reveal reality; deceiving a vendor into believing someone has offered you a better deal than they have; and more. Often, giving people a false impression borders on lying to them, and false impressions are sometimes created by lies of omission. Many people have made a lifestyle of giving false impressions to others: trying to impress friends at school, work, or while dating; shading the facts about how well they're doing; or hiding how poorly they're doing to secure favor or favors. According to THE BOOK, you cannot behave in this manner and expect God to bless any aspect of your life, including your business.

By THE BOOK Blessing

He who works deceit shall not dwell within my house; he who tells lies shall not continue in my presence. (Psalms 101:7)

By THE BOOK Lesson in Leadership

Hypocrites: Perfect Failures!

Jesus reserved some of his harshest words for people who gave false impressions—namely the hypocritical religious leaders: scribes and Pharisees. In fact, because Pharisees were in a leadership position, Jesus indicated that their condemnation was greater. In the twenty-third chapter of Matthew, Jesus gave dire warnings to the hypocritical Pharisees seven times. Here are three of the seven admonitions:

> Woe to you scribes and Pharisees, hypocrites! For you pay tithe of mint and anise and cumin, and have neglected the weightier matters of law: justice and mercy and faith.
>
> Woe to you, scribes and Pharisees, hypocrites! For you cleanse the outside of the cup and dish, but inside they are full of extortion and self-indulgence. Blind Pharisee, first cleanse the inside of the cup and dish, that the outside of them may be clean also.
>
> Woe to you, scribes and Pharisees, hypocrites! For you are like whitewashed tombs which indeed appear beautiful outwardly, but inside are full of dead men's bones and all uncleanness. Even so you also outwardly appear righteous to men, but inside you are full of hypocrisy and lawlessness. (Matthew 23: 23–28)

What's the significance of Jesus telling the scribes and Pharisees "woe" seven times? Bible scholars have long agreed that, in Scripture, seven symbolizes completeness or perfection. A few examples that drive this point home follow. On the seventh day God rested from his labors and creation was finished. Seven devils left Mary of Magdalene, signifying the totality of her previous possession by Satan. In the seventh year the Hebrew slave was to be freed, having completed his time of captivity and service. A search of the four gospels reveals that Jesus made seven statements from the cross before completing His perfect work on earth.

In addition, "seven times seven" reiterates the sense of completeness. Pentecost, the Feast of Weeks, is seven times seven days after Passover. "Seventy," which is literally "sevens" in Hebrew, strengthens the concept of perfection. There were 70 elders in Israel, and Jesus sent out 70 disciples to do His work. In Acts 6, the disciples chose seven to help serve. Israel was exiled to Babylon for 70 years to complete its punishment. The Lord was not giving Peter a mathematical number of times that he should forgive another person ("seventy times seven") but rather was insisting on perfect and complete forgiveness for a brother's sin. Thus, with the biblical significance of seven in mind, Jesus' seven woes to the hypocritical Pharisees were to classify them as perfect and complete failures in their leadership positions! His same seven "woes" should alert you to the dangers of hypocrisy, false impressions, and deceit.

Psalms 34:13–14 clearly states that deceitful false impressions are evil and that you must leave those ways behind if you want to run your life and business by THE BOOK: *"Keep your tongue from speaking evil and your lips from speaking deceit. Depart from evil and do good. Seek peace and pursue it."*

By THE BOOK Blessing

Definition of hypocrisy: Appearing to be on the outside something you are not on the inside.

YES/NO IS A NO-NO!

Sometimes, to play it safe, a leader will straddle the fence and give a yes/no reply rather than a straight answer. This seems innocent enough, until you realize what THE BOOK has to say about it.

> *But let your "Yes" be "Yes" and your "No" be "No." For whatever is more than these is from the evil one.* (Matthew 5:37)

Paul went on to say in 2 Corinthians 1:19–21: *For the Son of God, Jesus Christ, who was preached among you by us—by me, Silvanus, and Timothy—was not Yes and No, but in Him was Yes. For all the promises of God in Him are Yes, and in Him Amen, to the glory of God through us.*

So what's the big deal about giving a yes/no answer? It may leave a false impression to the person who asks the question. People often hear what they want to hear and, if you're not clear, they may assume something other than what you intended. This can eventually bring bitterness and resentment to the askers, especially if they feel you deceived them. The fact that yes/no answers can create bitterness and resentment is why Jesus said that they are from the evil one. In addition to potentially creating a false impression, yes/no answers must be revisited time and time again as you try to make a final and solid decision. Thus, they waste time and energy. So what are you supposed to say when someone asks you an awkward question or a question you're not sure how to answer? Don't answer it! It's far better to tell someone that you want to think or pray about an issue than to give a false impression that can potentially create hard feelings and misunderstandings. After telling someone that you want to think and pray about it, then think and pray about it!

To build a rock solid character, do the following:

1. Stop any misleading advertising that you engage in. If you're not sure whether or not it is misleading, then it probably is.
2. Stop spinning the feedback you give to make someone feel that they're doing either better or worse than they really are.
3. Stop misleading potential job candidates or employees about realities concerning compensation, advancement, future plans, and the like.

By THE BOOK Blessing

If you've given false impressions to others, follow the advice in James 5:16: *"Confess your trespasses to one another, and pray for one another, that you may be healed."*

Reconcile and Forgive Immediately!

Competitive business people are known for holding grudges. They begrudge employees who make mistakes, as well as those who leave their organization; they resent competitors who take away their business, as well as coworkers who wrong them and family members who don't support or appreciate their career endeavors. Some will make an effort to reconcile, whereas others nurse the grudge to their graves. At other times, they'll wait for another to reconcile with them, and in many cases, a person will reconcile but never really forgive. Jesus made clear the necessity to reconcile quickly:

> Therefore if you bring your gift to the altar, and there remember that your brother has something against you, leave your gift there before the altar, and go your way. First be reconciled to your brother, and then come and offer your gift. (Matthew 5:23–24)

The urgency Christ recommends is for good cause: if you have something against someone else, or they against you, bitterness, resentment, and anger will take root—causing you to sin. I wish I had followed the advice to stop what I was doing and reconcile several years ago when I was visiting my aging parents. My mother and I had endured a strained relationship for years. As her health was worsening and I was able to spend less time with her because of my travels, I had a strong compulsion to reconcile with her the final evening I spent at her home during my visit. She sat on a couch and I in a chair across the room. It was just her and me. The moment was perfect. I wanted to go over and tell her how sorry I was for the hard feelings that we had carried around and assure her that I cared for her and wanted to start over in our relationship. But for reasons I still cannot explain, I sat pat. The moment passed, others came into the room, and I determined that I would speak with her in the morning before they took me to the airport. That never happened. The next morning was hectic as I packed and left for the 90-mile trip from their mountain home to the Knoxville airport. As a result, I resolved to have my talk with her when I called the next Sunday. The

Saturday before I was to call her, my mother died. The guilt I carried in the wake of her death was even greater than the resentment and bitterness I felt during the years when we were estranged. When I finally said the words that had been on my heart, I spoke them to her as she lay in her coffin. I had missed the moment. This is why Matthew 5:23–24 makes so much sense and why Jesus stresses to do it now!

Based on what you've just read, some of you should put this book down. You have a phone call to make, a letter to write, or an old friend to visit to make things right. And it doesn't matter if you wronged them or if they wronged you. You should still make the first move to resolve your strained relationship. I know, I know. You may have to swallow your pride to make this happen. But don't let your pride stand in the way of a clear conscience and obedience to God's word. By the way, it matters not if the person you reach out to responds well to your reconciliation, because you're not only doing this for him or her. You're doing this for the health of your own soul, and as you demonstrate obedience you'll bring glory to God.

By THE BOOK Blessing

Forgive quickly. For those who continue to hurt you, pray for the qualities they seem to be lacking, and let God go to work on them.

BY THE BOOK LESSON IN LEADERSHIP

FAILING TO FORGIVE TORTURES YOU!

Strangely, many people think that by holding onto a grudge or by failing to forgive another person, they're getting even with them or hurting them. Wrong! You're killing yourself! Consider Jesus' parable of the unforgiving servant as related in Matthew 18:23 and 35:

Therefore the kingdom of heaven is like a certain king who wanted to settle accounts with his servants. And when he had begun to settle accounts, one was brought to him who owed him ten thousand talents. But as he was not able to pay, his master commanded that he be sold, with his wife and children and all that he had, and that payment be made. The servant therefore fell down before him, saying, "Master, have patience with me, and I will pay you all." Then the master of that servant was moved with compassion, released him, and forgave him the debt.

But that servant went out and found one of his fellow servants who owed him a hundred denari; and he laid hands on him and took him by the throat saying, "Pay me what you owe!" So his fellow servant fell down at his feet and begged him, saying, "Have patience with me, and I will pay you all." And he would not, but went and threw him into prison till he should pay the debt. So when his fellow servants saw what had been done, they were very grieved, and came and told their master all that had been done. Then his master, after he had called him, said to him, "You wicked servant! I forgave you all that debt because you begged me. Should you not also have had compassion on your fellow servant, just as I had pity on you?" And his master was angry, and delivered him to the torturers until he should pay all that was due to him.

So My heavenly Father also will do to you if each of you, from his heart, does not forgive his brother his trespasses.

Jesus went on to say in Matthew 6:12, *"forgive us our debts as we forgive our debtors."*

Based on these words from THE BOOK, one of your primary motivations to quickly forgive someone is so that you will also be forgiven from your own sins and not delivered to your torturers, as promised in the parable. What are the torturers that Jesus refers to? They are the diseases of the soul: fear, anger, bitterness, guilt, resentment, and lust. People who do not forgive others are carriers of these soul afflictions that rob their joy, peace, and love. Notice also that Jesus instructs to forgive from the heart. You have to mean it! And let me take some pressure off of you. Forgiving someone doesn't mean that you condone or accept as right what they did to you. Rather, it means that you release any bitterness or resentment you have toward that person. You don't hold it against him or her nor do you wish them harm. It means that you'll trust God to even the score if it needs evening, because although forgiveness is free, it is not cheap. There are consequences that we and others suffer for what we do to others, regardless of whether those we offend forgive us or not.

By THE BOOK Blessing

Forgiveness doesn't mean freedom from consequences. Jesus forgave Judas for betraying Him, but Judas' own torment and guilt drove him to commit suicide.

STOP CHASING THE SNAKE!

If a poisonous snake bites you, what should you do first: kill the snake or remove the venom? Many leaders choose to chase the snake to kill it, failing to realize that their actions only cause the venom to spread faster, causing a quicker death. The same holds true for those who fail to forgive. Rather than remove the venom and exercise forgiveness, they hold onto the poison and chase the snake, exacerbating their own inner torture during the process. But you must remember: by holding onto the venom, you're not hurting the snake; you're killing yourself!

This might be an appropriate time to do an inventory of grudges you're nursing, people you're resenting, and those with whom you must reconcile. It doesn't matter how far back the offense was. If you're carrying it around, it's affecting your performance more than you can possibly realize. Let it go. Chasing the snake is a race you cannot win.

To build a rock solid character, do the following:

1. Bring closure to past offenses. Identify amends you must make, with whom, and do it quickly.

2. Practice forgiving quickly. Realize that it is the responsibility of the more spiritually mature in a relationship to make the first move in restoration.

3. If someone continues to offend or hurt you, practice praying for them, the qualities they seem to be lacking. This follows the scriptural promise to bless your enemies and the promise to receive a blessing in return.

By THE BOOK Blessing

Finally, all of you be of one mind, having compassion for one another; love as brothers, be tenderhearted, be courteous, not returning evil for evil or reviling for reviling, but on the contrary blessing, knowing that you were called to this, that you may inherit a blessing. (I Peter 3:8–9)

SHINE THE LIGHT

Think of the character defects you dislike in people. If you're like the Apostle Matthew, you may despise most in others what you also see in yourself.

Matthew was a tax collector, and tax collectors were considered the vilest people in Israel. They purchased tax franchises from the Roman emperor for specific provinces so that they could turn around and tax the tar out of people. If you couldn't pay the tax man, he'd hire thugs to collect the debt. This breed was known for their selfishness, dishonesty, ruthlessness, and greed.

To fully grasp the low esteem that these men of ill repute were held in, it helps to know that the Jewish Talmud taught that it was considered righteous to deceive tax collectors! In fact, a tax collector like Matthew wasn't even allowed to enter the temple. This point is driven home in Jesus' parable of the Pharisee and the tax collector. Notice what I have bolded for emphasis:

Also, He spoke this parable to some who trusted in themselves, that they were righteous and despised others. Two men went up to the temple to pray, one a Pharisee and the other a tax collector. The Pharisee stood and prayed thus with himself, "God, I thank You that I am not like other men—extortioners, unjust, adulterers, **or even as this tax collector**. I fast twice a week; I give tithes of all that I possess." And the tax collector, **standing afar off** would not so much as raise his eyes to heaven, but beat his breast, saying, "God, be merciful to me a sinner!" (Luke 18:9–13)

A careful read of Matthew's gospel indicates that he despised hypocrites. Perhaps, this is because he had hated the hypocrisy of his own tax-collecting lifestyle before Christ called him. You see, despite Matthew's chosen profession, it appears that he was spiritually hungry and studied the Scriptures even though he wasn't allowed in the temple. In fact, Matthew quotes the Old Testament 99 times in his gospel; more than Mark, Luke, and John combined. There can be no question that his knowledge of God's expectations for right behavior caused conflict with the required daily practices of his job, causing him to see himself as a hypocrite. The strain of living with this tension can be severe. This may explain why he responded immediately to Jesus' invitation to follow Him: "*As Jesus passed on from there, He saw a man named Matthew sitting at the tax office. And He said to him, 'Follow Me.' So he arose and followed Him.*" (Matthew 9:9)

There are 27 mentions of hypocrites in the New Testament; 16 of those can be found in the Gospel of Matthew. Hypocrisy was a character trait that greatly offended Matthew; it was his primary pet peeve. What he judged most wrong in others once defined his own life. The same can be said for us.

If a judgmental, or proud, or unforgiving, or lying, or lustful, or angry person most offends you, it may very well be because you have problems with judging, pride, unforgiveness, lying, lust, or anger. Use the reaction you have toward the behaviors that appall you most in others as feedback to examine these same traits in your own life and further your life's endeavor to repent and build a rock solid character.

SUMMARY

Do you tell white lies? Do you keep commitments? Are you a second-miler? Do you give straight answers? Are you able and willing to reconcile and forgive quickly and from the heart? These are not rhetorical questions. The answers will help shape your entire essence as a leader and determine whether your personal foundation is built upon sand or stone.

REVELATION

For many of you, the fifth step—reconciling and forgiving immediately—will be the toughest. After all, how many times have you said or heard someone else remark: "I'll never forget the way he did . . ." or "I'll never forgive her for . . ." or even, "I forgive but I never forget." Frankly, the "forgive but not forget" phrase probably means that you've never really forgiven in your heart and still harbor bitterness toward your offender. Without question, the business trenches provide plenty of opportunities for leaders to become bitter: lost sales; credit they never receive; unjust blame they do receive in abundance; a coworker, customer, or vendor who lies or slanders them; and the list could go on until Christ returns. But perhaps the most dangerous grudge and poisonous venom is that which you hold for yourself: you can't forgive yourself for past mistakes, missed opportunities, a bad move, the wrong job, or disastrous decisions. For the same reason you fail to forgive others—to get back at them and make them suffer a while longer—you may be punishing yourself. "Stop chasing the snake" holds true when the snake is you, when your wounds are self-inflicted, when you are your own worst enemy, when no one has held you back but you still managed to find ways to self-destruct. Some of you wouldn't talk to your worst enemy the way you talk to yourself: "I'm such an idiot," "I blew it again," "I've wasted my life," "I can't do anything right!" If this is what you say when you talk to yourself, then it's time to knock it off and give yourself a break! You'll never be able to build strong relationships with others if you can't learn to live with yourself! The biggest reconciliation you may need to make is with yourself. Do it and send your torturers packing.

ACTION EXERCISE

FIVE STEPS TO BUILD A ROCK SOLID CHARACTER

Keep in mind the five character issues discussed in this chapter when completing the following:

1. Identify the character issues where you need the most work and list them here.

   _____

   _____

   _____

2. List one step you will take in each area to address this flaw.

   _____

3. List the top character flaw(s) in your key leader(s).

   _____

   _____

4. List one step you will take to bring this to their attention and help them address it.

   _____

CHAPTER 5

The "High Five" Principles to Elevate Your People Skills

GENESIS

Jesus was a people person! He walked slowly through the crowds and connected with others. He asked questions; He met needs; He displayed compassion and concern; and He maintained a servant's mindset throughout His ministry. Jesus demonstrated three critical success factors you must emulate to develop great people skills: (1) You must genuinely care about people. (2) Value people-work more than paperwork. (3) Learn to be efficient with things but effective with people. The five principles presented in this chapter will help you to elevate your people skills, regardless of their current state. I label them "High Five" because they are high-road principles that put others first.

Two of the great inhibitors to developing people skills are pride and arrogance. In fact, if you have "pit bull" people skills, you're probably selfish. Your love of self leaves little room for others. If this describes you, you must change your heart toward people! Enhanced people skills are essential to running your business by THE BOOK. They help you to build stronger workplace relationships and serve as a catalyst for higher morale, enhanced teamwork, and employee retention.

As a leader, you have the responsibility to use the workplace as a platform to positively impact others and help them reach their potential. But you are only able to maximize this opportunity if you have the people skills necessary to convert employees from compliant subordinates into committed followers. Without these skills, you are likely to rely on rules rather than relationships to get things done and reap a banquet of going-through-the-motions mediocrity. Sadly, non-relational bosses breed a brood of followers who feel more like personnel than people. These bosses make themselves too busy with administrivia to spend time with people, opting instead to pore over reports, crunch numbers, and send hourly e-mail directives. They build and maintain only surface relationships with their employees because they don't truly value them as individuals — seeing people primarily as automatons necessary to get the job done, a means to an end called *profit*. And although profit is important, the pursuit of it should not make relational casualties of your people. In fact, you'll find that the more you love money, the less you'll love your people.

The fact that Christians could assume an ineffective and unhealthy outlook toward human beings in the workplace runs totally contrary to the attitude Christ projected when interacting with people. Christ came to impact, to sacrifice, to meet needs, to teach, and to serve. We are to imitate His example. The good news is that with intent and dedication, great people skills *can* be developed. Once your heart is right, motives are pure, and mindset is humble, you'll be well-positioned to learn and apply the "High Five" for elevating your people skills as presented in this chapter. In the process, you'll become more charismatic, respected, and esteemed. As a result, you'll convert your employees from feeling like driven stakes into thinking and acting like stakeholders.

THE "HIGH FIVE" PRINCIPLES TO ELEVATE YOUR PEOPLE SKILLS

DON'T TALK TOO MUCH!

Three of the most important lessons I've learned about building relationships with people are: (1) relationships are built by dialogues, not monologues; (2) big leaders monopolize the listening while small leaders monopolize the conversation; and (3) people don't commit to you when they understand — they commit to you when they feel understood, and the only way that they can ever feel understood is when you zip your lips and listen to them!

By restraining your urge to talk too much, you accomplish three vital objectives:

1. You're less likely to say something foolish, reckless, boastful, or sinful. Consider Proverbs 10:19: *"In a multitude of words, sin is not lacking. But he who restrains his lips is wise."*
2. You're more likely to be considered as thoughtful and intelligent. Memorize Proverbs 17:25 before your next meeting: *"He who has knowledge spares his words, and a man of understanding is of a calm spirit. Even a fool is counted wise when he holds his peace; when he shuts his lips he is considered perceptive."*
3. You're not as likely to embarrass yourself as explained in Proverbs 18:13: *"He who answers a matter before he hears it, it is folly and shame for him."*

Even after you've determined to restrain your speech and listen more, you must employ these strategies:

1. Listen with the intent to understand and not to reply. People can tell when you're holding your breath and biting your tongue waiting for them to finish so that you can speak. To build great people skills, learn to hang onto their every word. Ask questions about what they're saying to clarify your understanding and withhold judgment until you're sure you've heard everything they have to say.

2. Don't interrupt people or finish their sentences for them. This is not only rude, it's disrespectful. Even though Jesus knew people's thoughts before they spoke them, there is no record of Him ever cutting people off in midsentence.

3. Don't steal their ego food. When someone tells you about something they did well or that went right, don't steal their thunder by topping what they said with something that you—or someone else—did that was better. When the 70 followers of Christ returned from their mission to tell Jesus that they were able to cast out demons in His name, He didn't say, "Ah, beginner's luck!" Rather, He rejoiced with them (Luke 10:18–19)!

By THE BOOK Blessing

Keep in mind that, when communicating, less is more. This is especially true when it comes to talking about you. You develop charismatic people skills when you take focus off of yourself and put it on the other person. Lack of charisma says, "Here I am," whereas highly charismatic people take the attitude, "There you are!"

Learn to Lead with Questions

As you are climbing up the leadership ladder, you are paid primarily for coming up with the right answers. However, the higher you go in leadership, the more you'll gain a greater return by learning to ask the right questions. Questions engage others and put a value on their contribution. Questions show that you care. Questions demonstrate that you don't believe you know it all. Questions exhibit humility. Questions help you determine where someone's heart or mind is at.

Effective questions that hone your people skills and help you engage others are: "Where do you see that I can make a greater contribution?" "How can I help you become more successful?" "What can we do to enhance teamwork?" "How can we make it easier for customers to do business with us?" "What do we do here that's dumb?" "What could we do to make it easier for new hires to get off to a faster start when they join our company?"

Asking questions gives you an opportunity to practice listening. Listening gives you a chance to practice silence. Silence gives you the time to practice thinking before replying. Thinking before replying will augment the value of your response and make it less likely that you say something you must apologize for later.

By THE BOOK Blessing

"He who can no longer listen to his brother will soon no longer be listening to God, either."

—Dietrich Bonhoeffer

Closing Thoughts on Not Talking Too Much

You will draw more people to you with a ready ear than with a loud voice. Engaging others earns influence, enhances charisma, and establishes trust. Engaging people makes you an engaging person.

DON'T KEEP SCORE

It's difficult to demonstrate that you value someone if you appoint yourself scorekeeper for their mistakes, offenses, and failures, rehearsing them in your mind while routinely reminding them of their humanity. Pride will also cause you to keep score of the favors you've done for others versus what they have failed to do for you in return: "I drove him there four times and he only gave me gas money once," "I bought her a Brighton handbag and she got me a balloon bouquet," "I gave him three qualified referrals and he sent me a guy so broke that he couldn't finance cheese for his Whopper." Whether you're tracking mistakes or tallying inequities, you're building a foundation for resentment that erects a wedge between you and others that makes connecting with them difficult and building a relationship nearly impossible.

By THE BOOK Blessing

So let each one give as he purposes in his heart, not grudgingly or of necessity; for God loves a cheerful giver. (2 Corinthians 9:7)

By THE BOOK Lesson in Leadership

Let God Keep Score

In the Book of Deuteronomy, God instructs His leaders and all of Israel to imitate His generosity and grace. At the end of every seventh year, every Israelite was to cancel debts owed by fellow citizens. If they would indeed cancel debts, model graciousness and forgiveness, and care for the poor, He would favor their land with abundant crops and freedom from invasion. God's instruction here provides us with a reminder of the nature of true leadership. Don't waste energy keeping score with people. Just give and God will keep score. Some people are tightfisted with time, money, resources, advice, and the like; they feel if they give it away, they are diminished, and there is less left for them. But just as when a candle lights another candle its light is multiplied rather than lessened, your impact and influence as a leader expands as you give the time, attention, respect, a ready ear, favor, and the resources necessary to build up your people.

By THE BOOK Blessing

Bear one another's burdens, and so fulfill the law of Christ. (Galatians 6:2) Do not be deceived, God is not mocked; for whatever a man sows, that he will also reap. (Galatians 6:7)

Keep your motives in check. When you do for others, first and foremost do so to remain obedient to God. Don't worry about who notices or who remembers. God notices and remembers. Part of becoming better at serving others is forgetting your service.

DON'T JUDGE

Many times Christians have a tough time connecting with non-Christians in the workplace. They can become judgmental and stand-offish. Imagine the Herculean task of trying to develop great people skills and affect others if your worldview is to judge others and bring them condemnation rather than compassion, understanding, and relationship. How do you connect with those who may not share your values? First, here are some ideas on what *not* to do:

1. Don't judge others and feel it necessary to point out their sins.
2. Don't make a big deal out of your own spiritual disciplines.
3. Don't try to debate someone into Christianity.

Somehow, many Christians have the idea that unless they jump all over non-Christians and condemn their sins, they imply approval of their lifestyles. Not at all! Everyone who gets to know you will soon become aware of what you don't do and would not do. But you're not supposed to judge non-Christians for their behavior. In fact, you're to expect defective behaviors from those who don't know Christ, as Paul points out in 1 Corinthians 5:9–13, where he advocates not keeping company with fellow Christians who behave poorly—not with nonbelievers!

> I wrote to you in my epistle not to keep company with sexually immoral people. Yet I certainly did not mean with the sexually immoral people of this world, or with the covetous, or extortioners, or idolaters, since then you would need to go out of the world. But now I have written you not to keep company with anyone named a

brother, who is sexually immoral, or covetous, or an idolater, or a reviler, or a drunkard, or an extortioner—not even to eat with such a person.

Paul clearly indicates that you should expect more from other Christians than nonbelievers. He also instructs that you should focus more on the humble task of judging yourself, rather than of judging others: *"For if we judge ourselves, we would not be judged"* (1 Corinthians 11:31). He also writes: *"Examine yourselves as to whether you are in the faith. Test yourselves"* (2 Corinthians 13:5).

What you should do is associate and connect with "wicked" folks when, in good conscience, you can show by your holy and happy life that there is an alternative. You need to be the kind of person unsaved people turn to as an alternative—not turn away from as an aggravation or annoyance. When you have a chance to tell someone about your faith, don't be legalistic, complex, or academic. Instead, just relate what Christ means to you, how you came to know Him, and how your life has changed since you put Him at the center. Be real. If you pretend to act holy, all that others will see is your posturing. But if you are real with others—if you don't hide your fears, your doubts, your weaknesses, your struggles—they will know that you are real. This transparency draws others to you, gives you a chance to influence and impact them, and makes you a far more effective people person.

One more thought: To enhance your people skills and workplace charisma, be more of a partier than a party-pooper, greeting others with an uplifting attitude, always ready to listen to them, advise them, and lend a helping hand. Don't be a killjoy, where you are always walking around with a condescending glare and judging the less spiritual. Your daily prayer should be that when people see what you do and hear what you say, that they will see less of you and more of Jesus. It was Christ's compassion and care for others that drew them to Him. Follow His example and you will attract and develop a team that follows you anywhere and through anything.

By THE BOOK Lesson in Leadership

The "Speck-Bone" Is Connected to the "Plank-Bone"!

When you judge someone for being prejudiced, could it be because you struggle with prejudice yourself? If a proud person rubs you the wrong way, might it be because he reminds you of your own arrogance? When you mock someone for losing their cool, is it because his behavior recalls for you the times you shamefully did the same? When you encounter a manipulator, is your ire aroused because she reminds you of when you found it necessary to manipulate others? Does someone's failure to admit an error grind your nerves because you become convicted of your own cover-ups and tendency to blame? "Yes" is probably the most appropriate and honest answer to all of these questions. The speck you judge in someone else's eye may very well be a reflection of the plank in your own eye.

Jesus had sage advice concerning the tendency to judge someone else's speck in their eye while you carry a plank of a like sin around in your own eye:

> Judge not, that you not be judged. For with what judgment you judge, you will be judged; and with the measure you use, it will be measured back to you. And why do you look at the speck in your brother's eye, but do not consider the plank in your own eye? Or how can you say to your brother, "Let me remove the speck from your eye," and look, a plank is in your own eye? Hypocrite! First remove the plank from your own eye, and then you will see clearly to remove the speck from your brother's. (Matthew 7:1–5)

The plank and speck as referred to in this passage are understood to be identical sins, only of different degrees. Based on these words, is Christ telling you to not try and help another with their obvious shortcomings? Not at all. He's instructing you not to judge them because of the shortcomings. And when you do attempt to "help" it's important that you assume the role of

111

a surgeon and not that of a judge. A surgeon brings healing. A judge brings condemnation. A surgeon skillfully removes the speck from an eye so that the person can see clearly and function at 100 percent efficiency. A judge doesn't bring healing; he brings guilt. In fact, some managers use guilt as their primary motivational tool without realizing that it is not motivation at all—but manipulation.

2 Samuel 12:1–7 tells how Nathan the prophet was sent by the Lord to tell King David a parable about how a rich man with many flocks and herds refused to feed a traveler from his own abundance but instead took and killed the one and only lamb of a poor man to prepare for the guest. David's anger was greatly aroused against the rich man, and he said to Nathan, "As the Lord lives, the man who has done this shall surely die! And he shall restore fourfold for the lamb, because he did this thing and because he had no pity." Then Nathan said to David, "You are the man!" Nathan used the parable to convict David of his own sin in having Uriah the Hittite killed and taking his wife Bathsheba.

Could it be that David was so angered and judgmental toward the speck in the rich man's eye who had everything in the story and who took from the poor man with nothing because he had the larger plank of a like sin in his own eye as a result of committing the same offense? To David's credit, he repented and declared, "*I have sinned against the Lord*" (2 Samuel 12:13).

To upgrade your people skills, you should use your temptation to judge aspects of someone else's life as a wake-up call to first go on a plank-hunt within your own life and repair yourself before you endeavor to become someone else's "Mr. or Mrs. Fix It." Then, check your motives before you coach or correct the person and make sure that your feedback and redirection are based on discernment with the goal of healing and not rooted in judgment with guilt as your goal. You might also give the person you're ready to judge some benefit of the doubt by assuming the best about them rather than the worst. When my wife, Rhonda, was struggling to get answers concerning her credit card account, the customer service representative helping her made promises to respond to her inquiries but then failed to do so. Exasperated by the lack of communication, Rhonda left a pointed voice mail message expressing her displeasure with the unprofessional treatment she had received. The next day, the rep called to humbly apologize and explained that she had been out of the office for several days due to her young daughter's sudden death and subsequent funeral. Rhonda felt awful and learned a powerful lesson about assuming the best, rather than the worst, about someone and why they do something. To this day she will reply, "You don't know what they might be going through today," when someone cuts her off in traffic or fails to deliver on a deadline.

By THE BOOK Blessing

You cannot connect with people if you condemn them. Nor can you impact them if you avoid them. You reach people by giving energy and attention to what you have in common and not by how you differ. Find the 1 percent of common ground you both stand on, and give that 1 percent 100 percent of your focus.

See others as they can be, not just as they are, and realize that your job as a leader is to help them make up the difference.

CONTROL YOUR ATTITUDE AND EMOTIONS

Here are three things you should remember to help build your people skills: (1) you can't be persuasive when you're abrasive; (2) people have a tough time buying into you when you're a screamer, a whiner, a naysayer, a hothead, a bully, or a basket case; and (3) leaders are expected to be more emotionally mature, measured, and mannerly than followers. It comes with the territory and with the biblical mandate that to whom much is given, much is required (Luke 12:48).

Regardless of what happens to you, you are responsible for how you respond. While you may not be able to control the provocation or the event, you remain responsible for choosing the right response to it.

This is why it's wrong to say, "You gave me a bad attitude" or "That meeting gave me a bad attitude." Nothing can give you a bad attitude. You choose a bad attitude. To improve your people skills, you must improve the choices you make in response to what happens to you and around you.

By THE BOOK Blessing

He who is slow to wrath has great understanding, but he who is impulsive exalts folly. (Proverbs 14:29)

The discretion of a man makes him slow to anger, and his glory is to overlook a transgression. (Proverbs 19:11)

BY THE BOOK LESSON IN LEADERSHIP

MOSES' POOR CHOICE COST HIM THE PROMISED LAND

What a shame. Moses had led the nation of Israel out of Egypt and held them together—an estimated two million of them—for 40 years as they wandered the wilderness waiting to enter the Promised Land only to be prohibited by God from completing his mission. Why? Disobedience and doubt brought on by his lack of emotional control.

> Now there was not water for the congregation; so they gathered together against Moses and Aaron. And the people contended with Moses and spoke saying, "If only we had died when our brethren died before the Lord! Why have you brought up the assembly of the Lord into this wilderness, that we and our animals should die here? And why have you made us come up out of Egypt, to bring us to this evil place? It is not a place of grain or figs or vines or pomegranates; nor is there any water to drink." So Moses and Aaron went from the presence of the assembly to the door of the tabernacle of meeting, and they fell on their faces. And the glory of the Lord appeared to them.

Then the Lord spoke to Moses, saying, "Take the rod; you and your brother Aaron gather the congregation together. Speak to the rock before their eyes, and it will yield its water; thus you shall bring water for them out of the rock, and give drink to the congregation and their animals." So Moses took the rod from before the Lord as He commanded him.

And Moses and Aaron gathered the assembly together before the rock; and he said to them: "Hear now you rebels! Must we bring water for you out of this rock?" Then Moses lifted his hand and struck the rock twice with his rod; and water came out abundantly, and the congregation and their animals drank.

Then the Lord said to Moses and Aaron, "Because you did not believe Me, to hallow Me in the eyes of the children of Israel, therefore you shall not bring this assembly into the land which I have given them." (Numbers 20:2–12)

Some may wonder what all the fuss was about. It doesn't seem to be that big of a deal that Moses struck the rock twice rather than speaking to it as he was instructed by God. He had followed God's instructions and struck the rock back in the seventeenth chapter of Exodus to get water under similar circumstances. And didn't he have the right to react angrily to his whiney, doubting followers? Evidently not. Moses' lack of emotional control led to disobedience and doubt. And because God expects more from His leaders, Moses suffered severe consequences for his poor choice. God would allow him to climb a mountain and sneak a peak of the Promised Land he had endeavored 40 years to enter, but he would not lead his people into it.

By THE BOOK Blessing

He who is slow to anger is better than the mighty, and he who rules his spirit than he who takes a city. (Proverbs 16:32)

Five Proverbs to Improve Your Attitude

1. The first of these five Proverbs is a warning. Awareness of it should help make you more intentional with self-control:

   "Whoever has no rule over his own spirit is like a city broken down, without walls." (Proverbs 25:28)

2. The second is instructional and is instrumental in defusing tense situations:

   "A soft answer turns away wrath, but a harsh word stirs up anger. The tongue of the wise uses knowledge rightly, but the mouth of a fool pours forth foolishness." (Proverbs 15:1)

3. The third reminds you to choose your battles and encourages you not to wrestle with pigs lest you also get dirty:

   "Do not answer a fool according to his folly, lest you also be like him." (Proverbs 26:4)

4. The fourth Proverb establishes the impact that those whom you choose to associate with can have on your own emotional state:

   "Make no friendship with an angry man, and with a furious man do not go, lest you learn his ways and set a snare for your soul." (Proverbs 22:24)

5. The fifth Proverb encourages you with a key benefit of a great attitude:

   "All the days of the afflicted are evil, but he who is of a merry heart has a continual feast." (Proverbs 15:15)

By THE BOOK Blessing

Which attitude will you choose to begin each day: "Good morning, God!" or "Good God! Morning?"

The quality of your people skills will be greatly determined by your attitude toward people and situations. Never forget that attitude is a choice, and the quality of your leadership is greatly dependent upon the quality of your choices. To better control emotional reactions and more effectively connect with followers, follow the advice of James 1:19: *". . . let every man be swift to hear, slow to speak and slow to wrath."*

LOVE YOUR NEIGHBOR

One of the key themes in this chapter on how to elevate your people skills is that you won't be able to do so until you genuinely care about people. Executing the four points given previously will help you demonstrate a healthy love for others at work. Without a genuine love for the people you work with and for your customers and their needs, you'll be inclined toward selfishness, greed, and harshness rather than demonstrating the selfless, gentle, servant mindset demonstrated by Christ. But who is your neighbor, and what exactly does it mean to love your neighbor in the workplace?

1. **Look for ways to meet their needs.** 1 Corinthians 10:24: *"Let no one seek his own but each the other's well being."*

   Turf wars, jockeying for position, and backstabbing are terms as common in some businesses today as quarterly report, human resources, and mission statement. Needless to say, you'll have a tough time improving your people skills if the hand you pat people on the back with has a knife in it. The truth is that if you don't love your neighbor like you should, it is probably because you don't love God as you should. That's why in Matthew 22:37 Jesus identifies the two great commandments in the order they're listed. Unless you love God first, you'll be unable to love your neighbor as yourself:

   Jesus said to him, *"You shall love the Lord your God with all your heart, with all your soul, and with all your mind. This is the first and great commandment. And the second is like it: You shall love your neighbor as yourself."*

2. **Speak respectfully to them and well of them.** Ephesians 5:29: *"Let no corrupt word proceed out of your mouth, but what is good for necessary edification."*

Planting seeds of discord, spreading or listening to gossip or rumors, conducting the "meeting after the meeting," and reveling in "If I were in charge around here" conversations disrespects others and diminishes yourself. The people you work with know that if you talk about others, you'll also talk about them. This truth does little to enhance your people skills and increase your influence in their eyes. On the other hand, when you are loyal to those not present, you earn the respect and trust of those who are.

3. **Provide the resources they need to be successful.** Matthew 5:1–2: *"And seeing the multitudes, He went up on a mountain, and when He was seated His disciples came to Him. Then He opened His mouth and taught them saying ..."*

   If you have capable employees and you don't invest in their development, then you deserve to lose them. In fact, you probably will. And if they do continue to work for you, you don't deserve results from them because you're expecting the prize without paying a price. Author and speaker Zig Ziglar put it well: "There is one thing worse than training people and having them leave. It's not training them and having them stay!"

4. **Care enough to confront them when they're off track.** Matthew 26:34: *"Jesus said to him, 'Assuredly, I say to you that this night, before the rooster crows, you will deny Me three times.'"*

   Even though it can be unpleasant, you must care enough about your people to confront them when they're off track. Temporary discomfort is better than temporary ease if it averts permanent failure. Don't let society's politically correct tendency to sugarcoat, trivialize, marginalize, sanitize, and compromise cause you to let people live in a gray area where they know neither right nor wrong, winning nor losing, success nor failure. When you confront someone firmly, with tact and compassion, they come to trust your motives and appreciate that with you, they know where they stand.

5. **Pray for them.** Luke 22:31: And the Lord said, *"Simon, Simon! Indeed, Satan has asked for you, that he may sift you as wheat. But I have*

prayed for you, that your faith should not fail; and when you have returned to Me, strengthen your brothers."

When you pray for your people, ask that God shows you how He is working in their lives and how you can be a part of His plan. Pray also for the qualities they seem to be lacking and may need more of to become more successful. When you pray for someone, you will begin to look at them differently—as God sees them. This perspective will be a catalyst to connecting with them, becoming more relational, and leading them to higher performance levels.

By THE BOOK Blessing

To give love, you must first have it. If your relationships with others aren't what they should be, you can rest assured that your relationship with God is not what it should be.

WHO IS MY NEIGHBOR?

Leave it to a lawyer to look for a loophole! After Jesus affirmed him for admitting that he should love his neighbor as himself, the lawyer wanted to justify himself—and most likely the fact that he had *not* been neighborly to some—and said to Jesus, "And who is my neighbor?"

Then Jesus answered and said:

> A certain man went down from Jerusalem to Jericho, and fell among thieves, who stripped him of his clothing, wounded him, and departed, leaving him half dead. Now by chance a certain priest came down that road. And when he saw him he passed by on the other side. Likewise, a Levite, when he arrived at the place, came and looked and passed by on the other side. But a certain Samaritan, as he journeyed, came where he was. And when he saw him, he had compassion. So he went to him and bandaged his

wounds, pouring on oil and wine; and he set him on his own animal, brought him to an inn, and took care of him. On the next day, when he departed, he took out two denarii, gave them to the innkeeper, and said to him, "Take care of him; and whatever more you spend, when I come again, I will repay you." So which of these three do you think was the neighbor to him who fell among the thieves?

And he said, "He who showed mercy on him."

Then Jesus said to him, "Go and do likewise." (Luke 10: 30–37)

To fully appreciate this well-known parable, there are three things you must consider:

1. The priest and Levite were coming from Jerusalem on the same day, indicating that they had probably worshipped at the Temple. These men had just come from church but still found it easy to ignore a half-dead human lying naked on the road. Great people skills, eh?

2. Samaritans were despised by the Jews. They were thought to have demons (John 8:48–49). Jesus used the little regarded Samaritan in this parable to make a powerful point. It was society's lowly outcast who offered help to one who had probably harbored prejudice against him, while the "respected" men of the cloth walked on by. The Samaritan saw through whatever label he may have applied to his Jewish oppressor and had compassion on him as his neighbor.

3. A denari was approximately one day's wages. Thus, the Samaritan not only gave up two day's pay to help the man, he personally bandaged wounds, pouring oil and wine on them. He put him on his own animal while he walked and took him to an inn. He likewise promised to pay more if the bill exceeded what he had given. The Samaritan didn't just write a check and go his way. He got his hands dirty, incurring personal inconvenience and expense to care for this stranger, his neighbor.

This parable offers a broad picture of who your neighbor is in the workplace: "Us" in our own department, as well as "them" across the hall. It covers everyone under your roof, as well as those in branch offices. It also includes the prospects and customers who make it possible for you to receive that paycheck every two weeks. You should also include the vendors who service your organization. When you start looking at everyone as your neighbor, it takes the pressure off because you don't have to pick and choose to whom you'll be kind, respectful, or decent. You can do just as Christ did and love them, warts and all. Oh, you may find some of them hard to like. But you can still love them.

By THE BOOK Blessing

Assuredly, I say to you, inasmuch as you did it to one of the least of these My brethren, you did it to Me. (Matthew 25:40)

Assuredly I say to you, inasmuch as you did not do it to one of the least of these, you did not do it to me. (Matthew 25:45)

STRATEGY

Grasp that one of the great paradoxes of God's world is that when you take your focus off your own wants and needs and put it on the wants and needs of others, more of your own wants and needs are met!

SHINE THE LIGHT

One of the benefits of developing great people skills is that it makes you more approachable. People are drawn to those who listen, who don't keep score, who are nonjudgmental, who control their emotions, and who act in a loving manner toward others. Naturally, these benefits will evoke substantial benefits as you interact with both coworkers and customers.

Although apostles like John, James, and Peter had the highest profiles among Jesus' team, I believe that Andrew may have had some of the most effective people skills. Andrew is mentioned only twelve times in the Bible and never again after Pentecost. He also lived perpetually in the shadow of his better-known brother, Peter. In fact, Andrew met Jesus first, and brought Peter to Jesus, but never seemed to mind playing second fiddle to his brother "The Rock."

Throughout his time with Jesus, and even after Christ's death, Andrew focused more on individuals than on capturing crowds. He also showed that he was a man of action, whose love for people allowed him to both engage others and be sought by them.

- One of the two who heard John (The Baptist) speak and followed Him was Andrew, Simon Peter's brother. He first found his own brother Simon and said to him, "*We have found the Messiah. And he brought him to Jesus*" (John 1:40–41).
- One of His disciples, Andrew, Simon Peter's brother, said to Him, "*There is a lad here who has five barley loaves and two small fish . . .*" (John 6:8–9).
- Now there were certain Greeks among those who came up to worship at the feast. Then, they came to Philip, who was from Bethsaida of Galilee, and asked him saying, "Sir, we wish to see Jesus." Philip came and told Andrew, and in turn Andrew and Philip told Jesus (John 12:20–22).

The story of the Greeks coming to Philip raises an interesting question that also points to Andrew's approachability and people skills: why didn't Philip bring the Greeks to Jesus himself?

It seemed that Andrew had, among all the disciples, earned the reputation of bringing people to Jesus. He remained committed to this right up until the very moment when he died on a cross. While the Bible says nothing about Andrew after Pentecost, church history and its historians offer insight concerning his ministry. Here is what they tell us:

1. Andrew and Peter perhaps remained as ministry partners for two decades after Pentecost, taking numerous journeys together.[1]
2. Andrew preached in regions ranging from Armenia to the northern shores of the Black Sea and into Asia Minor.[2]
3. Peter and Andrew probably split up in Patrae, with Peter going on to Rome and Andrew remaining in Patrae. Patrae was located on the northern shore of a large peninsula known as the Peleponnesus, which was connected to the Greek mainland only by the tiny isthmus of Corinthia.[3]
4. Andrew aroused the anger of Patrae's governor by healing his ill wife who subsequently converted to Christianity. The governor's brother also converted, but Aegeates, the governor, wanted nothing to do with the new religion and considered his wife's conversion as an alienation of affection.[4]
5. As a result, Andrew was imprisoned. However, Andrew's skill at impacting others, one-on-one, caused his jailers to be changed constantly, since they were converted almost as soon as they were assigned to the apostle. Finally, Aegeates gave orders that Andrew be crucified.[5]
6. Andrew was tied rather than nailed to a cross, so that he would die a slow, lingering death of exposure and exhaustion. The crucifixion took place on the seashore, as the governor expressed hope that Andrew would be gradually torn apart by the wild dogs that foraged about that area.[6]
7. Andrew's approachability, nonjudgmental attitude, ability to control his emotions, and love for his neighbor allowed him to remain effective for Christ unto his death. While dying on the cross, the now 60-plus-year-old apostle preached to a gathering crowd that was possibly larger than he had preached to during prior decades of ministry. The *Acts of Andrew* report that in the days he spent slowly dying, the apostle converted over 2,000 onlookers, mostly by having conversations with those who, one at a time, approached

this unique apostle who practiced his ability to connect with people even unto his last breath.[7]

SUMMARY

You may be born with a personality that makes connecting with people easier for you, but ultimately people skills are more a result of a right heart than a buoyant personality. All five disciplines listed in this chapter start with selflessness. Because of this, the path to greater people skills runs through your heart, not your genes or your head.

REVELATION

Perhaps the best job description found in the Bible for anyone wanting to develop their people skills is in Romans 12:9–18. It covers and expands the "High Five" principles covered in this chapter:

> Let love be without hypocrisy. Abhor what is evil. Cling to what is good. Be kindly affectionate to one another with brotherly love, in honor giving preference to one another; not lagging in diligence, fervent in spirit, serving the Lord; rejoicing in hope, patient in tribulation, continuing steadfastly in prayer, distributing to the needs of the saints, given to hospitality.
>
> Bless those who persecute you; bless and do not curse. Rejoice with those who rejoice and weep with those who weep. Be of the same mind toward one another. Do not set your mind on high things, but associate with the humble. Do not be wise in your own opinion. Repay no one evil for evil. Have regard for good things in the sight of all men. If it is possible, as much depends on you, live peaceably with all men.

ACTION STEPS

THE "HIGH FIVE" FOR ELEVATING YOUR PEOPLE SKILLS

Which of the "high five" people skills are you best at? For the five strategies listed, rank your skills on a scale of 1 to 5, with 5 the highest score.

Strategy – Don't talk too much.
Your ranking: _____

Strategy – Don't keep score.
Your ranking: _____

Strategy – Don't judge.
Your ranking: _____

Strategy – Control your attitude/emotions.
Your ranking: _____

Strategy – Love your neighbor.
Your ranking: _____

CHAPTER 6

Four Keys to Create Life-Work Balance

GENESIS

The most concise section in my *How to Run Your Business by THE BOOK* seminars concerns the connection between life balance and effectiveness on the job. It is also the section that attendees commend as one of the most helpful. As a result of this feedback, I've spent more time writing and speaking on this vital connection and how to become more balanced in four key areas of life: mental, emotional, physical, and spiritual.

I readily admit that I can never recall my life being in what I would characterize as "perfect" balance. In fact, I would assert that ever expecting oneself to arrive at or spend much time in such a blissful state may not be a reasonable expectation this side of heaven. However, the good news is that reaching a place in your life where you find yourself in perfect balance is not the point. Rather, it is the committed *pursuit* of this balance that will greatly determine the quality of your life.

Many hard chargers in business wrongly believe that after they make enough money, it will be easier to balance their lives. This is a false philosophy because once you make money your idol, you will sacrifice family, God, health, and self to obtain it—throwing your life further out of balance! As you'll discover in this chapter, THE BOOK provides a path that suggests you are far more likely to obtain and enjoy material things *after* you prioritize balance in your life and not before. In other words, you should expect that your pursuit of balance will precede material increase rather than believe that greater balance will result because you have accumulated more in your life that is material.

Often you hear about so-and-so who "worked long and hard" and burned out. However, it's safe to say that we all know plenty of folks who have worked long and hard but never burned out. This is because long, hard work is not the cause of burnout. Stress is the cause of burnout. And there is little that causes more stress than when long, hard work causes you to live your life out of balance for any period of time. Undue stress chews you up and spits you out, and without a prioritized and balanced life, more "stuff" brings increased stress, not less of it.

The four key areas this chapter will cover for building a balanced life are not equal in importance. Spiritual balance ranks as the most essential component of balance to pursue; without it, mental, emotional, and physical balance are irrelevant because any level of attainment will be fleeting without a spiritual foundation. Without God at the center of your life, you'll become prideful, selfish, and arrogant, destroying any chance of attaining or maintaining mental or emotional balance; and, void of God, your unrepentant sin will weaken and diminish you mentally, physically, and emotionally.

Without question, when you are mentally, physically, emotionally, and spiritually charged, you experience multiple benefits as a result: your attitude is elevated, your energy is expanded, your relationships are strengthened, your thinking is unclouded, your confidence is edified, your judgment is precise, your conscience is clear, and your job performance soars. Conversely, when you are out of balance in just one area of your life, aspects of your work life suffer as a result: loss of focus, passion, stamina, integrity, discernment, self-esteem, and so on.

With all that is at stake, don't wait until "someday" to begin to focus more on building a balanced life. Some of you have said "someday" long enough. "Someday" has become "one of these days," and "one of these days" puts you on track for "none of these days." There is power in *now*. There is no power in later, because later is never guaranteed. All you have is now!

BUILD MENTAL BALANCE IN YOUR LIFE

> The heart of the prudent acquires knowledge, and the
> ear of the wise seeks knowledge. (Proverbs 18:15)

For years, one of my most valued disciplines has been a personal growth program. A personal growth program is similar to an exercise program, only you work out your mind rather than your body. It may be something as simple as reading one book per month in your field. Just like a bona fide workout program, you must execute a personal growth program with intent; you can't just hope to find time for it. A personal growth program should be mandatory for all leaders because the growth of your team is contingent upon your own growth. After all, how can you export what you don't have or take your people on a journey you've never been on? Sadly, many leaders are losing their relevance because they haven't upgraded their skills and the business is passing them by. They're yesterday's news because, although they work hard on their job, they've stopped working on themselves. Somewhere along the line they got the idea that growth was automatic and that if they just showed, they'd grow; as a result they have plateaued.

The world's wisdom suggests that to get ahead in business, you should chase power, position, and money. Proverbs 16:16 suggests otherwise: *"How much better to get wisdom than gold! And to get understanding is to be chosen rather than silver."*

Along these lines, I have for years counseled young people entering the business world to *not* chase money. I tell them instead to chase the right skills, wisdom, knowledge, habits, and attitudes, and then the money will chase them. I remind them that in order to get more than they've got, they must become more than they are; the *becoming* has to happen first! In a society and in an age addicted to a lottery mindset it is common and comical to witness how many misguided instant-gratification addicts attempt to get more even though they haven't become more growth-wise since they left school!

It's common to see a business person become successful and then use the tax return for their highest-ever income as a permission slip to never read another book. They point to their past success and use it as justification to stay exactly as they are. What results is a "been there and done that" attitude that labels them as a know-it-all burdened by an "intelligence arrogance" that eventually becomes a disabling ignorance. Although arrogance is bad enough, dumb *and* arrogant push the envelope! Soon these "wise in their own eyes" leaders have to spend more time at work trying to get done what they could have accomplished in far less time had they worked smarter rather than harder. As they spend more time at work, they have less time to spend with their families and friends, and on their health and spiritual development. This creates stress that makes them even less effective at work, resulting in more frustration and more hours spent in the workplace. This cycle of viciousness has been the culprit behind incalculable dismissals, divorces, heart attacks, addictions, suicides, plateaus, breakdowns, and broken families.

A commitment to personal growth helps replace the cycle of viciousness with a cycle of virtue. This is because as you work on yourself and upgrade your skills, you become better at what you do. As a result, you don't have to spend as much time on the job getting your work done. This means that you can take your days off and leave work when you're supposed to, and build a life of balance with family, friends, health, and God. The improvements in these aspects of your life leave you less stressed and more fulfilled. When you bring the power of these traits back into the workplace with you, you become even more effective—accelerating results and the impact you have as a leader. This brings us to a moment of truth: Which cycle are you riding—viciousness or virtue? The good news is that you get to choose. The bad news is that, because you get to choose, you can't blame anyone but yourself for being caught up in the life-draining, destined-to-be-deadly cycle of viciousness.

By THE BOOK Blessing

How long, you simple ones, will you love simplicity? For scorners delight in their scorning, and fools hate knowledge. (Proverbs 1:22)

By THE BOOK Lesson in Leadership

King Solomon's Mind

King Solomon, the third king of Israel, ruled for 40 years. He was the son of King David and Bathsheba, and reigned in the years around 961 to 922 B.C. Proverbs, Ecclesiastes, and Song of Solomon are books of the Bible that are attributed at least partially to his authorship. While his father, David, was a great military leader, Solomon never had to lead an army, as peace reigned during his rule. He probably became king at around 18 years old, while David was still alive and ailing. The book of 1 Kings tells of a pivotal moment in the young king's life when he chose wisdom of the mind and heart over all other choices for what he desired from God:

> At Gibeon the Lord appeared to Solomon in a dream by night; and God said, "Ask! What shall I give you?" (1 Kings 3:5)

Can you imagine how most people would respond to this question? They'd probably treat God like a genie that popped out of a bottle and present him with a five-page list of demands ranging from fur coats to Ferraris! Here's how Solomon answered:

> "Therefore give to Your servant an understanding heart to judge Your people, that I may discern between good and evil. For who is able to judge this great people of Yours?"
> The speech pleased the Lord, that Solomon had asked this thing. Then God said to him, "Because you have asked this thing, and have not asked long life for yourself, nor have asked

riches for yourself, nor have asked for the life of your enemies, but have asked for yourself understanding to discern justice, behold, I have done according to your words; see I have given you a wise and understanding heart, so that there has not been anyone like you before you, nor shall any like you arise after you. And I have also given you what you have not asked; both riches and honor, so that there shall not be anyone like you among the kings all your days. So if you walk in My ways, to keep My statutes and My commandments, as your father David walked, then I will lengthen your days." (1 Kings 3:9–14)

Solomon's wisdom attracted wealth unlike what any man before or since has accumulated. Solomon's fortune in today's dollars has been estimated at over five hundred billion dollars. The following passage helps explain why:

. . . So King Solomon surpassed all the kings of the earth in riches and wisdom.

Now all the earth sought the presence of Solomon to hear his wisdom, which God had put in his heart. Each man brought his present: articles of silver and gold, garments, armor, spices, horses, and mules, at a set rate year by year. (1 Kings 10:23–24)

The Queen of Sheba alone gave him one hundred and twenty talents of gold, spices in great quantity and precious stones! (1 Kings 10:10)

By THE BOOK Blessing

When your motives cause you to grow in wisdom for the sake of others, you capture God's favor. God will then give you favor with men.

Pursue mental balance by doing the following:

1. Commit to a personal growth program, and make time to do it. Turn off the television, put down the morning "doom-paper," and invest time upgrading and increasing your wisdom, knowledge, and understanding.
2. Pray for wisdom. Pray for the mind of God. Pray that God gives you sound judgment and precise discernment.
3. Apply what you learn. The purpose of personal growth is not to accumulate knowledge but to put it to use! Life doesn't reward what you know; it rewards what you do with what you know!

BUILD EMOTIONAL BALANCE IN YOUR LIFE

> These things I command you, that you love one another.
> (John 15:17)

Emotional balance concerns the strength and quality of relationships you have with friends, family, and coworkers. When relationships go bad, the ensuing stress and pain can be ongoing, tortuous, and, over time, unbearable. Relationships take work and must be sustained over time. Following the five strategies for building your people skills offered in Chapter 5 will help create a strong foundation for relationships at work and at home. As a reminder, the "High Five" principles were: not talking too much, not keeping score, refraining from being judgmental, controlling your attitude, and loving your neighbor.

Broken relationships often result from selfish motives. When one person in a relationship is the perpetual taker, the other party begins to feel used, manipulated, and underappreciated. The Proverb writer nailed it when he wrote: *"The leech has two daughters—give and give!"* (Proverbs 30:15). A one-sided relationship misses the mandate of Christ to put others first and meet their needs. How strong a relationship do you have with the person that you never hear from until they need something? Along the same lines, if you are the taker, don't be so naïve as to believe that the person whose pocket you pick, time you waste, passion you drain, and ear you exhaust hasn't figured out that your idea of a relationship is more of a "me"-lationship.

Gossip, not keeping secrets, and failing to be happy for your friend's successes while you neglect to empathize during their setbacks also impairs relationships. THE BOOK has great relational advice concerning these issues.

GOSSIP

> Where there is no wood, the fire goes out; and where
> there is no talebearer, strife ceases. (Proverbs 26:29)

This wisdom reminds you that "wood" is not only spewing gossip but also listening to and enabling it.

> But shun profane and idle babblings, for they will
> increase to more ungodliness. And their message will
> spread like cancer. (2 Timothy 2:16)

The "more ungodliness" referred to here covers everything from judgment, to white lies, to giving false impressions and more.

SECRETS

> A talebearer reveals secrets, but he who is of a faithful
> spirit conceals a matter. (Proverbs 11:13)
> He who covers a transgression seeks love, but he who
> repeats a matter separates friends. (Proverbs 17:10)

Some Christians have gotten pretty slick and use a sneaky strategy to both gossip and reveal secrets: "Don't let this go any further, but I understand that Bill and Kate are having marital problems because he was caught fooling around with his secretary. I tell you this so that you can pray for them." Check your motives before you betray confidences and gossip under the guise of "helping." Engaging in this nonsense may fool others, but it only diminishes yourself.

APPROPRIATE JOY AND EMPATHY

> Rejoice with those who rejoice, and weep with those who weep. Be of the same mind toward one another. (Romans 12:1)

This might be news to some leaders who withhold positive reinforcement in an attempt to keep their people on their toes and prevent them from becoming lazy, but your initial reaction to someone's success should not be to bring them back down to earth: "Don't let your great month go to your head. You'll be back down here with the rest of us in no time." Rather, you're instructed by THE BOOK to rejoice with those who rejoice. This should always be your first reaction to the success of another—spouse, offspring, friend, or coworker. If you feel the need to warn them about humility, then you should do it in a separate conversation and not immediately after their victory. Let them shine for the moment and don't steal their ego food!

At the same time, the last thing most people want in the immediate aftermath of something bad happening to them is a pep talk. Rather, weep with them first. Feel their pain and express understanding for their loss. After you've connected with them on this empathic level, they will be more receptive to your "look on the bright side" advice. In other words, when a friend tearfully tells you that her boyfriend just broke up with her, don't rattle off: "He's a loser anyway. You're better off without him!" Instead, convey that you're sorry for her loss, the pain she's feeling, and for what she is going through. After you've made the connection and validated her feelings of grief, it's more appropriate to begin pointing out new possibilities and the upside of losing the loser.

Obviously, gossiping, being indiscreet, and failing to rejoice with those who rejoice and weep with those who weep will cause you to earn the workplace reputation of one who brightens the room by leaving it. Your relationships are doomed to be superficial at best, while your trust and influence levels with others hover between anemic and pathetic. The same goes for your relationships away from work. The stress resulting from this emotional imbalance will adversely affect your own morale, performance, and peace of mind. The proposition is simple: to have true friends, you must act like a true friend. To enjoy the trust of others, you must protect their secrets, look out for their interests, add value to their lives, talk to them rather than talk about them, and share their victories as well as their defeats.

By THE BOOK Blessing

A friend loves at all times. And a brother is born for adversity. (Proverbs 17:17)

BY THE BOOK LESSON IN LEADERSHIP

THE LOVE AND RESPECT FORMULA FOR A ROBUST MARRIAGE

Perhaps the most pervasive form of emotional strife that impairs job performance results from stressful relations with one's spouse. Rather than return to an unhappy home, many people choose to spend more time at work, further exacerbating their marital distress. THE BOOK offers what is perhaps its most profound advice for a healthy marriage in Ephesians 5:33: *"Nevertheless let each one of you in particular so love his own wife as himself, and let the wife see that she respects her husband."* According to the Apostle Paul, what women want most from their husbands is love, and what men want most from their wives is respect. When a woman shows disrespect to her husband, he becomes less loving in return. This makes the woman even less respectful, and the man more withdrawn. It's a destructive cycle that creates substantial stress, strife, and eventual divorce. At the same time, when a man is unloving to his wife, she often respects him less, causing him to become even less loving, accelerating the cycle of marital doom. Don't misunderstand, women still want respect and men want love; it's just that love and respect are the two prime motivators for wife and husband, respectively.

A woman may say, "I'll respect him when he deserves it." In other words, she'll respect a man conditionally. But, at the same time, you can be assured that she expects him to love her unconditionally. The problem with this is that her attitude makes the man responsible for both the love and the respect! Although she may not respect some of the things her husband does, THE BOOK mandates that she still demonstrate respect for him as a human being; disrespect the performance but still respect the person as your husband. Whether you're a man or woman who is failing to get the respect or love you need, you can reverse the destructive cycle by giving your partner more of what they need and watch as, eventually, a reciprocal flow of what you need starts to come back to you. In his book *Love & Respect* (2004, Thomas Nelson), author Dr. Emerson Eggerichs makes a compelling case for the biblical requirement for love and respect in a robust marriage and offers steps to help each spouse deliver.

Pursue emotional balance by doing the following:

1. Protect your relationships by purifying your motives and taming your tongue.
2. Give your spouse what they most crave, even if you're not currently getting it in return. Your efforts can reverse a destructive cycle.
3. Schedule relationship-building activities into your calendar each week. Then work the rest of your schedule around these activities rather than trying to cram these essential activities into your schedule.

By THE BOOK Blessing

Husbands, love your wives, just as Christ also loved the church and gave Himself for her, that He might sanctify and cleanse her with the washing of water by the word. (Ephesians 5:25–26)

BUILD PHYSICAL BALANCE INTO YOUR LIFE

Or do you not know that your body is the temple of the
Holy Spirit who is in you, whom you have from God,

and you are not your own? For you were bought at a price; therefore glorify God in your body and in your sprit, which are God's. (1 Corinthians 6:19)

During a stretch in the 1990s, I would resolve each New Year's to get into shape and lose weight. To support my endeavor, I'd purchase the latest bestseller on the topic. Perusing the pages I would find nuggets like "eat smaller portions" or "reduce your fat intake" or "exercise at least 30 minutes four times per week." One day it occurred to me that I was well aware of the commonsense strategies presented in the books I read. I knew that I should eat less, eat healthier foods, and exercise in order to get into shape and lose weight. I did not suffer for lack of knowledge. I suffered for lack of doing what I knew. Frankly, when it came to eating right and exercising, doing right was a bit bothersome! Fortunately, my 6-foot 4-inch height made my 40 pounds of excess weight less noticeable, but I knew it was there. In addition to aggravating the ulcers I had at the time, my failure to live a healthy lifestyle made it awkward for me to discuss the importance of discipline, sacrifice, and self-respect with the people who worked for me.

What made my task tougher was the culture of the industry I was working within: the automotive retail business. Working in a car dealership is characterized by eating the wrong foods, in the wrong quantities, and at the wrong hours. We didn't eat throughout the day; we grazed. In fact, you can safely say that in many high-stress businesses, more people commit suicide with a fork than with a gun! To add insult to injury, the long hours and six-day workweeks left little time for exercise.

Then one day I discovered one of the world's greatest motivators: disgust. On the same morning that I found I could no longer button the coat of my favorite suit, I also realized that, as I drove the car, my idle arm rested comfortably on my stomach rather than in my lap. I'm not sure how long I had been in that condition; all I remember is that when I recognized my condition, being disgusted with myself motivated me more than any book I had ever read during my New Year's

Resolution quests to shape up. I decided at once to begin paying the price to convert my "caddy shack" into the temple that God expected it to be. As a result, I began to discover the power of discipline. To me, discipline had always had a negative connotation—like punishment of some sort. However, I've since discovered that discipline is simply making yourself do the things you know are important, even when you don't want to do them; once you do them long enough they become habits and no longer require the effort they did at the outset. Once I realized the results that eating better and exercising had on my health, energy, self-confidence, and leadership credibility, I recognized that I no longer looked at what I was doing as paying the price but as enjoying the price. Discipline bridges the gap that takes you from paying a price to enjoying it. Many people start but few finish what they begin because they lack discipline. They don't stick with something long enough to convert their new actions into healthy habits. Oftentimes, they lack a big enough "why." Nazi concentration camp survivor Victor Frankl suggested that you could live with any "what" or "how" as long as you have a big enough "why." The "why" is your purpose for taking action and subjecting yourself to the pain of discipline so that you don't have to one day suffer from the pain of regret. This is what writer E.M. Gray meant when he wrote: "Successful people have made the habit of doing things failures don't like to do. Successful people don't like to do these things either. But they subordinate their dislike to the strength of their purpose. The strength of their purpose propels them toward their dreams, forcing them to do the things they don't really want to do so they can obtain the things they really want to have."

What is your "why" for building your body into a temple worthy of the God who dwells there? A longer life? Obedience to God's word? Greater self-esteem and confidence? Increasing your leadership credibility so that you can more effectively impact others? Increased energy and health? All of the above? The more reasons the better, because the bigger the "why," the easier the "what" and "how."

By THE BOOK Blessing

For no one ever hated his own flesh, but nourishes and cherishes it, just as the Lord does the church. (Ephesians 5:29)

By THE BOOK Lesson in Leadership

A Perfect Seven for Better Health

Following are seven insights from THE BOOK concerning health and the quest for physical balance. You are never too young or old to begin shaping up your temple in a manner that demonstrates gratitude and respect for it as one of your greatest gifts. In the process, you'll build a physical machine that adds stamina, energy, confidence, and credibility to your leadership in the workplace.

1. **Don't disqualify yourself!** *"Do you not know that those who run in a race all run, but one receives the prize? Run in such a way that you may obtain it. And everyone who competes for the prize is temperate in all things. Now they do it to obtain a perishable crown, but we for an imperishable crown. Therefore I run thus; not with uncertainty. Thus I fight: not as one who beats the air. But I discipline my body and bring it into subjection, lest, when I have preached to others, I myself should become disqualified."* (1 Corinthians 9:24–27)

2. **Tend to the temple!** *"Do you not know that you are the temple of God and that the Spirit of God dwells in you? If anyone defiles the temple of God, God will destroy him. For the temple of God is holy, which temple you are."* (1 Corinthians 3:16–17)

3. **Do unto God!** *"Therefore whether you eat or drink, or whatever you do, do all to the glory of God."* (1 Corinthians 10:31)

4. **Eat to live. Don't live to eat!** *"Blessed are you, O land, when your king is the son of nobles, and your princes feast at the proper time—for strength and not for drunkenness."* (Ecclesiastes 10:17)

5. **Attitude influences health!** *"A merry heart does good, like medicine. But a broken spirit dries the bones."* (Proverbs 17:22)
6. **Hatred and bitterness destroy health!** *"Better is a dinner of herbs where love is, than a fatted calf with hatred."* (Proverbs 15:17)
7. **The importance of rest!** *"Then the apostles gathered to Jesus and told Him all things, both what they had done and what they had taught. And He said to them, 'Come aside by yourselves to a deserted place and rest a while.' For there were many coming and going, and they did not even have time to eat. So they departed to a deserted place in the boat by themselves."* (Mark 6:30–32)

By THE BOOK Blessing

I can do all things through Christ who strengthens me. (Philippians 4:13)

Pursue physical balance by doing the following:

1. Develop the discipline to be temperate in all things.
2. Create a big enough "why" to make the "what" and "how" of building your temple manageable, desirable, and enjoyable.
3. Rest. Fatigue will sour your disposition as it makes you a coward and a pessimist, and impairs your judgment, making you more susceptible to sin.

BUILD SPIRITUAL BALANCE INTO YOUR LIFE

> Now it came to pass in those days that He went out to the mountain to pray and continued all night in prayer to God. (Luke 6:12)

Spiritual balance concerns the quality and depth of your relationship with God. It is the bedrock that makes improvement in all other areas of your life measurable and sustainable. Thus your pursuit of spiritual balance must be a priority! Galatians 5:16–18 tells us that you have two

141

natures warring for control over your life: the old sinful nature of the flesh and the Spirit. Which nature will win? The one that you feed the most!

How do you know if you're out of spiritual balance? For starters, you feel increasingly stressed. While this is often the first clue, the root cause goes deeper, because when you feel stress, it indicates that you've lost your sense of gratitude. Frankly, it's nearly impossible to be grateful and unduly stressed simultaneously.

BE THANKFUL IN ALL THINGS

There are at least four good reasons why we should give thanks for whatever God allows to happen in our business and in our lives. When times are tough, giving thanks is tougher, but an even greater measure of your faith is remembering to offer glory and gratitude to God when everything is going your way and you are tempted to forget about God. Being thankful in all things is an essential spiritual discipline that enhances spiritual balance in your life. To accelerate its development, consider and apply the following four truths:

1. God is in control of all things. Nothing happens without His awareness and permission, not even the falling of one sparrow. Therefore, we can be sure that God is fully aware of everything that happens to us.

   > Are not two sparrows sold for a copper coin? And not one of them falls to the ground apart from your Father's will. But the very hairs of your head are all numbered. Do not fear therefore; you are of more value than many sparrows. (Matthew 10:29–31)

2. THE BOOK tells you that if you work according to God's will, then everything will work out for your good.

   > And we know that all things work together for good to those who love God, to those who are called according to His purpose. (Romans 8:28)

3. One of the highest purposes for which God allows difficulties in our lives is to conform us to the image of Christ. As you learn to respond as Christ would to whatever situations you face at work or away, you develop His characteristics, including patience, endurance, compassion, discernment, wisdom, humility, self-control, and many other important qualities.

4. God wants to teach you His thoughts and ways, which are higher than your thoughts and ways. By humbling yourself and thanking God for whatever He allows you to experience, you will demonstrate humility.

> For My thoughts are not your thoughts, nor are your ways My ways," says the Lord. "For as the heavens are higher than the earth, so are My ways higher than your ways and My thoughts than your thoughts. (Isaiah 55:8–9)

Zig Ziglar wrote, "The more you are grateful for, the more you'll have to be grateful for." Without a doubt, gratitude seems to attract more blessings, just as ingratitude and entitlement appear to repel it. A great way to gain perspective and take an inventory of your daily blessings is by keeping a gratitude journal. *The Simple Abundance Journal of Gratitude* (1996, Grand Central Publishing) by Sarah Ban Breathnach is a great tool for this purpose. As you log your daily blessings, which may range from getting an ideal parking space to landing the big account, you'll develop a sense of gratitude toward men and God that improves your attitude and makes you even more "bless-able." I've kept a gratitude journal for seven years, taking it with me even when I travel. It has become a faith-building discipline and a daily tribute to what is right in the world and in my life.

By THE BOOK Blessing

Rejoice always, pray without ceasing, in everything give thanks; for this is the will of God in Christ Jesus for you. (1 Thessalonians 5:16)

How Can Busy People Make Time for God?

In the midst of balancing work and family obligations, how can busy people make time for God: for prayer, Bible reading, and other devotional time? First, you can be sure that you'll rarely *find* time for these essential disciplines. This fact should alarm you, because the farther you drift from God's word, the harder it is to hear His voice. When you don't hear God, you'll depend more on your own wisdom for business and family decisions and less on the infinite wisdom of God. I don't need to tell you the kind of disaster this brings about! The Bible talks about how Jesus rose early and went off by Himself to pray in a solitary place (Mark 1:35). His example is worth following. Get the devotional fires burning early in the morning—in the quiet and without interruptions. Another strategy is to seize your commute time to listen to devotional messages or to meditate on or memorize Scripture.

Commute time probably accounts for the greatest amount of wasted time in our culture. The government estimates that the average American worker commutes about 25 minutes to and from work. That's nearly an hour in the car each weekday. If you used that time to listen to an audio recording of the Bible, you'd get through the entire Bible in three months! You'd also be less likely to get angry, impatient, or depressed listening to the horrific daily news stories. Listening to Scripture will also make traffic jams far more meaningful as you might just hear the word you need to solve a problem for yourself or someone else.

The Bible says in James 4:8 that if you draw near to God, then He will draw near to you. It doesn't say you can just drift there or hope you get lucky and end up in His presence. Drawing near indicates a deliberate and focused effort on your part. If you intend to keep God at the center of your life as you face daily challenges and opportunities, then *making* the time to draw near to Him is not optional—it's mandatory.

By THE BOOK Blessing

"Return to Me," says the Lord of hosts, and "I will return to you," says the Lord of hosts. (Zechariah 1:3)

By THE BOOK Lesson in Leadership

Spiritual Disciplines: A Cause and an Rx for Depression

Like stress, depression is an indicator that you've lost your spiritual balance. Much of depression is the result of running out of emotional energy. It can be used up on either good or bad activities—on the heels of either great accomplishments or colossal failures.

Elija and Jonah used up their emotional energy to bring about major revivals. In both instances, their success was followed by suicidal depression. The following Scriptures describe the immediate aftermath of their great successes:

> And Ahab told Jezebel all that Elija had done, also how he had executed all the prophets with the sword. Then Jezebel sent a messenger to Elija, saying, "So let the gods do to me, and more also, if I do not make your life as the life of one of them by tomorrow about this time." And when he saw that, he arose and ran for his life, and went to Beersheba, which belongs to Judah, and left his servant there.
>
> But he himself went a day's journey into the wilderness and came and sat down under a broom tree. And he prayed that he might die, and said, "It is enough! Now, Lord, take my life, for I am not better than my fathers!" (1 Kings 19:1–4)

Jonah:

> And it happened, when the sun arose, that God prepared a vehement east wind; and the sun beat on Jonah's head, so that he grew faint. Then he wished death for himself, and said, "It is better for me to die than to live." (Jonah 4:8)

Many business leaders today are so busy renewing, reviving, and building their organizations that they've spent no time renewing, reviving, and building up themselves! They've been so busy with production that they haven't rebuilt their personal capacity to produce.

We are all subject to get off track and occasionally abandon spiritual disciplines like prayer, Bible study, Scripture meditation, and Christian fellowship. These disciplines are essential to sustaining spiritual and emotional energy, and disconnecting from them for too long leaves you empty and depressed. At this time, it would be useful to reevaluate the spiritual disciplines in your own life necessary to building or sustaining the emotional and spiritual energy you'll need to not only survive but to thrive at home and at work in these challenging times.

By THE BOOK Blessing

As the deer pants for the water brooks, so pants my soul for you, O God. My soul thirsts for God, for the living God. (Psalms 44:1-2)

Pursue spiritual balance by doing the following:

1. Seek God first with the confidence that when you do so in earnest, all other things will be added to you. *"Seek first the Kingdom of God and His righteousness, and all these things shall be added to you"* (Matthew 6:33).
2. Use a gratitude journal to battle stress by creating a perspective of daily thankfulness.
3. Develop spiritual disciplines like morning prayer, Scripture meditation, church fellowship, and the like to feed your spirit and arm yourself to fight off the carnal nature that battles for control of your mind, will, and emotions. One of my favorite spiritual disciplines is taking the Daily Success Course via e-mail as offered free by the Institute in Basic Life Principles. This 49-week course covers the 49 general commands of Christ and explains how to apply them in your life. It's a very effective way to learn about the Bible in only 10 minutes per day. You can enroll for free at Iblp.org.

SHINE THE LIGHT

Just as many organizations attempt to build a great brand and then fail because they perform with excellence only occasionally, you cannot build greatness into your life until you consistently incorporate balancing disciplines into your daily routine. Consistency of performance separates the benchwarmers from the All Stars, the flashes-in-the-pan from the legends, in any endeavor. Frankly, even the most sloth and reckless individuals can manage to do what is productive occasionally, on the good days, when they feel like it. But those who are truly committed to worthy endeavors—and achieving a successful work-life balance is one of the most essential—discipline themselves to do what is most important, even when it is not pleasant, convenient, easy, or without cost.

To create a robust work-life balance, you must go beyond good intentions, "trying it out," or getting off to a fast start by doing the right things for a few days and then backsliding. Rather, you will need to elevate living with balance beyond "whim" status and commit to making it a lifestyle. Just as Paul exhorted Timothy to run his race with endurance, you must do the same. Disciplining yourself so that you can endure in your pursuit of balance and make it a lifestyle means that:

1. You trade in what's temporal for what's eternal.
2. While others are seduced by emergencies of the moment, you commit to priorities.
3. You plan and execute rather than react.
4. While others spiral down, you step up.
5. You eagerly pay the price because you value the prize.
6. While others discuss, you decide.
7. You mind the Lord's business, knowing that He will see to yours.
8. While others make excuses, you solve problems.
9. You eagerly pursue heavenly things and leave your earthly cares with the Lord.
10. While others drift off, you turn it on.
11. You do what others aren't willing to do, so you can enjoy what few ever achieve.
12. While others are distracted by the allure of instant gratification, you persist in the face of difficulties, embracing that "why" you're doing

what you're doing justifies the "what" and "how" you endure to secure it.

Incredibly, some leaders are not interested in committing to mental, emotional, physical, and spiritual disciplines because they feel that the effort required restricts and burdens them. They couldn't be more wrong. Discipline does not restrict, it liberates. Discipline doesn't diminish your options, it expands them. The more disciplined you become in the four key areas discussed in this chapter, the more opportunities you'll have to elevate your own life and positively impact others. In fact, the alternative to discipline is disaster.

SUMMARY

The quest for mental, emotional, physical, and spiritual balance is not a destination but a lifetime journey. As with any long trip, you are likely to get off course from time to time. The faster you recognize deviations and correct your course, the more your overall performance will improve. In fact, a letup in any one of the four areas covered will adversely affect your overall performance. For instance, when your health gets out of whack, it will affect your relationships. When your relationships sour and create stress, it adversely affects your health and mental state. Let your spiritual sector get too far off track and you become one big mess in no time! Conversely, an improvement in any of the four areas has the potential to positively impact your overall performance in each sector. Because a balanced life is vital to both your personal and your work life, you cannot afford to neglect productive disciplines that feed your spiritual nature. Incorporate daily and weekly activities to address each arena, and then schedule them. When you truly commit to balancing your life, you're able to work rather than be worked, and able to live rather than be lived.

REVELATION

Perhaps the two most effective words to finding balance in your life are "be there." When you're at home, *be there!* When you are spending time with your family or are on vacation, *be there!* And when you're at work, *be there*, too! Fully engage yourself wherever you are at the moment because one of life's most draining and stressful activities is to be one place physically and somewhere else mentally.

As a business leader you must enlarge your goal beyond earning well to living well. You must go past trying to add years to your life and add life to your years. After all, what good does it do you to become rich but sick, rich but alone, rich but spiritually bankrupt? Remember the words of Jesus:

> Then He spoke a parable to them, saying: "The ground of a certain rich man yielded plentifully. And he thought within himself saying, 'What shall I do, since I have no room to store my crops?' So he said, 'I will do this: I will pull down my barns and build greater, and there I will store my crops and my goods. And I will say to my soul, 'Soul, you may have many goods laid up for many years; take your ease; eat, drink, and be merry." But God said to him, 'Fool! This night your soul will be required of you; then whose will those things be which you have provided?'
>
> "So is he who lays up treasure for himself, and is not rich toward God." (Luke 12:16–21)

ACTION EXERCISE

FOUR KEYS TO CREATE WORK-LIFE BALANCE

1. Evaluate the four key areas of balance and rank each sector, placing a "1" in the blank where you believe you have the strongest balance at this time, a "2" in the second highest area, and so forth.
   ____ Mental: personal growth and continual learning.
   ____ Emotional: the health of your relationships in your personal and business life.

_____ Physical: physical balance; the care you take of your body.
_____ Spiritual: the strength of your relationship with God as evidenced by your ongoing spiritual disciplines.

2. List one step you'll take to improve balance in each sector, and be very specific.

A. Mental:

_____

B. Emotional:

_____

C. Physical:

_____

D. Spiritual:

_____

CHAPTER 7

How to Manage Your Money by THE BOOK

GENESIS

Many Christians don't like to talk about money, especially when it comes to giving it. Some biblical principles concerning finances make them uncomfortable and fearful. However, THE BOOK speaks about money often, and so did Jesus. More than 2,350 verses of the Bible deal with money or possessions, as do 16 of Jesus' 38 parables. There is no need to fear what THE BOOK has to say about money, because God's financial laws are not designed to punish or restrict us but to bless us when we understand and apply His principles.

I have discovered that many people like to play dumb when it comes to knowing what God says about managing money. Debt is a curse? I am supposed to tithe? I should avoid business partnerships? But wouldn't God understand that in business we have to do that to make a profit? There are consequences for robbing God? I shouldn't co-sign a loan for a friend? The procession of prattling could proceed for pages.

This chapter provides THE BOOK's insight and answers to four important questions about finances. This may be one of this book's most important chapters for many readers, as the pursuit of business success can tempt you to depart from God to pursue money. You can go from being independently wealthy to independent of God. Most business people would be horrified at the thought of being labeled as one who pursues idols. Yet money and success can become your idols when you begin to give them more attention and affection than you give to God.

We live in an age of obscene and extreme materialism and consumerism. In such times, God can be expected to send economic crises to force our attention back to Him as our Source and free us from the idols we've chased and worshipped. Business leaders are some of the worst perpetrators of material idolatry as they embezzle, misuse, and abuse money and trust to enrich themselves. Witness the rising number of enterprises once thought invulnerable now rendered as impotent or insolvent, while their leaders are shamed, broken, and sometimes jailed. Through an economic meltdown, God releases the prideful and greedy from the possessions that possess them. Sadly, this is the only way He can turn some folks back from their reckless quest to build earthly treasures at the expense of heavenly riches. Jesus' words when speaking to the wealthy but complacent Laodicean church are more relevant today than ever:

> I know your works, that you are neither cold nor hot. So then, because you are lukewarm, and neither cold nor hot, I will vomit you out of My mouth. Because you say, "I am rich, have become wealthy, and have need of nothing"—and do not know that you are wretched, miserable, poor, blind and naked. (Revelation 3:15–17)

Contrary to the claim of many, money is not the root of all evil. Declaring such nonsense perverts the Scripture, which says, *"For the love of money is the root of all kinds of evil, for which some have strayed from the faith in their greediness, and pierced themselves through with many sorrows"* (1 Timothy 6:10). Frankly, money can be the root of all good when earned with the right heart and used as God intends. But make no mistake about it: you cannot be wrong with money and right with God. If this chapter disturbs and convicts you, it is because it has much to teach you. If you're able to discard some of the conventional thoughts you have about finances and keep an open mind, you'll find that biblical principles concerning finances for your personal and business life make great sense. You'll be even more delighted to discover how well they work when you apply them!

What Does THE BOOK Say About Earning and Giving Money?

Throughout THE BOOK, money is found to be a prime competitor with God for our attention and affection. In fact, God sets the record straight concerning the origins of prosperity early on in the Book of Deuteronomy, as well as the tendency for it to make us forget about Him.

A. **It is God who gives the power to earn or obtain wealth.** *"And you shall remember the Lord your God, for it is He who gives you power to get wealth"* (Deuteronomy 8:18).

Perhaps this is why Paul set out to humble the "haves," lest they feel superior to the "have-nots" with his words: *"For what makes you different from another? And what do you have that you did not receive? Now if you did indeed receive it, why do you boast as if you had not received it?"* (1 Corinthians 4:7).

B. **God realizes the danger of you becoming self-sufficient once you prosper.** His words to the early nation of Israel stand as warnings for us today:

> Beware that you do not forget the Lord your God by not keeping His commandments, His judgments, and His statutes which I command you today, lest—when you have eaten and are full, and have built beautiful houses and dwell in them; and when your herds and your flocks multiply; and your silver and your gold are multiplied;

when your heart is lifted up, and you forget the Lord your God who brought you out of the land of Egypt, from the house of bondage; who led you through that great and terrible wilderness, in which were fiery serpents and scorpions and thirsty land where there was no water; who brought water for you out of the flinty rock; who fed you in the wilderness with manna, which your fathers did not know, that He might humble you and that He might test you, to do you good in the end—then you say in your heart, "My power and the might of my hand have gained me this wealth." (Deuteronomy 8:11–17)

By THE BOOK Blessing

No servant can serve two masters; for either he will hate the one and love the other, or else he will be loyal to the one and despise the other. You cannot serve God and mammon [wealth]. (Luke 16:13)

The picture is clear: whatever we have comes from God. The warning is also to the point: don't let the blessings you receive from God cause you to forget about Him. With this in mind, you can understand why giving is so highly touted and demanded throughout THE BOOK. After all, you're only giving back to God a portion of what is His in the first place; by giving to Him and others, you are demonstrating that your dependence is still on God and not on the temporal things that can make you proud and independent.

Twelve Points of Giving

1. **You'll receive in proportion to how you give.** Giving begrudgingly or out of a sense of obligation totally misses the point. Give for the joy of helping others and making a difference, not because you feel that you have to. Sometimes your dire financial situation may convince you that it makes no sense to give because, on paper, you

cannot afford it. This is when you must remember that giving is not a logical issue of the head but a character issue of the heart. It's a chance to demonstrate faith, obedience, and compassion, and to have your needs met in return by God.

> There is one who scatters, yet increases more; and there is one who withholds more than is right, but it leads to poverty. The generous soul will be made rich, and he who waters will also be watered himself. (Proverbs 11:24)
>
> But this I say: He who sows sparingly will also reap sparingly, and he who sows bountifully will also reap bountifully. So let each one give as he purposes in his heart, not grudgingly or of necessity; for God loves a cheerful giver. (2 Corinthians 9:6)

2. **Jesus is watching your giving habits.** The widow who gave her last two mites to the church treasury is one of the best known stories in THE BOOK. What the widow gave as an offering that day was impressive not only because of what she parted with but because of what she had left after giving it—nothing! The story of the widow's two mites took place near the end of Jesus' life. Note that while Jesus was in the temple, He was not speaking or preaching at this particular moment. Rather, He had positioned himself to sit and watch what people brought to the temple to give. Because Hebrews 13:8 tells us that Jesus is the same yesterday, today, and forever, you can be certain that He is watching your giving habits as well—as little reveals more about the state of your heart than what you give away and what you decide to keep for yourself.

> Now Jesus sat opposite the treasury and saw how the people put money into the treasury. And many who were rich put in much. Then one poor widow came and threw in two mites, which makes a quadrans. So He called his disciples to Himself and said to them, "Assuredly, I say to you that this poor widow has put in more than all of those

who have given to the treasury; for they all put in out of
their abundance, but she out of her poverty put in all that
she had, her whole livelihood." (Mark 12:41–44)

3. **Giving to God should be a priority, and not what is left over after everything else is paid.** This means that when you tithe—giving 10 percent of all your increase—that you should tithe off of the gross and not the net! Make excuses for not doing this if you like, but pencil-whipping God is probably not a good idea!

> Honor the Lord with your possessions and with the first-fruits of all your increase; so your barns will be filled with plenty, and your vats will overflow with new wine. (Proverbs 3:9–10)

4. **Failing to pay God your tithes and offerings robs Him.** Don't think for a moment that God wants you to tithe because He needs your money. He doesn't. What He is concerned with is the condition of your heart that allows or prevents you from being able to be obedient and part with a portion of what He gave you in the first place! It's a bit astounding how many Christians, who profess to trust Christ for their salvation, won't trust Him with their finances!

> Will a man rob God? Yet you have robbed Me! But you say, "In what way have we robbed You?" In tithes and offerings. (Malachi 3:8)

5. **The only time God asks us to test Him throughout the entire Bible is in the area of giving.** This is because tithing is designed to benefit you, not God! He wants you to develop your faith to the point where you are able to cheerfully release some of the prosperity He sent your way and be blessed by having your needs met again as a result! Give 10 percent of your personal income as well as 10 percent of your business profits. If you give more than 10 percent or donate time, expertise, clothing, or other materials, these are not

considered part of the tithe but are regarded as offerings, which are what you give over and above the tithe.

> Bring all the tithes into the storehouse, that there may be food in My house. And try Me on this, says the Lord of hosts, "If I will not open the windows of heaven and pour out for you such blessing that there will not be room enough to receive it." (Malachi 3:10)

6. **Tithing is not just "Old Testament Law" but is mandated by Christ.** A common excuse for not tithing is that it is mandated in the Old Testament but not in the New Testament. This is simply not true. Nowhere in the New Testament will you find the tithe rescinded. In addition, Jesus clearly said you should tithe.

> Woe to you, scribes and Pharisees, hypocrites! For you pay tithe of mint and anise and cumin, and have neglected the weightier matters of the law; justice and mercy and faith. These you ought to have done, without leaving the others undone. (Matthew 23:23)

If Christ clearly instructs you not to leave something undone, it's quite obvious that He expects you to do it!

7. **Failing to give according to God's laws causes you to depart from Him.** Disobedience always causes a separation between you and God because it is sin. Although you may never intentionally depart from the presence, protection, and blessings of God, you do so nonetheless when you disobey Him.

> Yet from the days of your fathers you have gone away from My ordinances and have not kept them. Return to Me and I will return to you, says the Lord of hosts. But you said, "In what way shall we return?" Malachi 3:7

Take a look back at point 4—Malachi 3:8—to understand how the people in question departed from God.

157

8. **God may choose to frustrate our own efforts to have our needs met if we don't pay attention to His church or His people in need.** In Malachi 3:9–11, God promises to rebuke the devourer for those who tithe:

> "And I will rebuke the devourer for your sakes, so that he will not destroy the fruit of your ground, nor shall the vine fail to bear fruit for you in the field," says the Lord of hosts; "And all nations will call you blessed, for you will be a delightful land," says the Lord of hosts.

This promise also means that He may choose not to rebuke the devourer for those who are disobedient, resulting in a curse on your current efforts to prosper. In fact, the lack of blessing in any area of your business or your life is often evidence of a curse against that part of your business or your life, brought about by disobedience.

> You are cursed with a curse because you have robbed me . . . (Malachi 3:9)
>
> Now therefore, thus says the Lord of hosts: "Consider your ways! You have sown much, and bring in little; you eat, but do not have enough; you drink, but you are not filled with drink; you clothe yourselves, but no one is warm; and he who earns wages, earns wages to put into a bag with holes. . . . You looked for much, but indeed it came to little; and when you brought it home, I blew it away." "Why?" says the Lord of hosts. "Because of My house that is in ruins, while every one of you runs to his own house. Therefore the heavens above you withhold the dew, and the earth withholds its fruit." (Haggai 1:5–9)

9. **Don't listen to men or philosophies that create their own rules for giving.** An attendee to my workshop told me that her pastor told the poor members of the church that they could pay a half-tithe. I asked for her to give me the Scripture that states what her pastor told her. She could not. The pastor was wrong to add to God's

158

words, nor should she have embraced man's wisdom because it was easier for her than being obedient to God.

> Every word of God is pure; He is a shield to those who put their trust in Him. Do not add to His words, lest He rebuke you and you be found to be a liar. (Proverbs 30:5–6)

10. **Try as you may, you cannot buy off God.** Giving tithes and offerings doesn't excuse or cancel out other sins! Many people give out of guilt. They cheat a customer or employee, so they put a little extra in the offering plate. If this describes you, then you would be well advised to save your money and get your heart right!

> For I desire mercy and not sacrifice; knowledge of God and not burnt offerings. (Hosea 6:6)
> To do righteousness and justice is more acceptable to the Lord than sacrifice. (Proverbs 21:3)

11. **If your prime motive is to make money and accumulate wealth, then these things will never satisfy you.** This explains why those who build their lives around the material and arrive at millionaire or billionaire status often find themselves with the emptiness of a kid who opens his last present on Christmas morning and wonders, "Is this all there is?"

> He who loves silver will not be satisfied with silver; Nor he who loves abundance with increase. This also is vanity. (Ecclesiastes 5:10)

12. **Your motive for giving should be to bring glory to God and not for personal recognition.** This is the advantage of giving to other Christians as a priority; they will thank God and give glory to Him. It is important that you deflect the praise of others whom you help and direct their thanks to God. Ideally, give anonymously whenever you can. This is why Christ instructed us to give secretly, pray

secretly, fast secretly . . . *"and your Father, who sees in secret, shall reward you openly"* (Matthew 6:1–18).

> Let your light so shine before men, that they may see your good works and glorify your Father in heaven. (Matthew 5:16)

What's Tithing Got to Do with Leadership?

A business owner recently asked me why I felt it necessary to spend so much time covering the issue of tithing in a *How to Run Your Business by THE BOOK* seminar that I had conducted for 45 members of his leadership team. His main point was "what has tithing got to do with leadership?" I thought that his question was both excellent and appropriate. Since I have also become convinced that if one person asks a question many others are thinking the same thing, I want to briefly address this topic here. So, what does tithing have to do with leadership?

- Tithing demonstrates obedience and the humility to put God first. These are essential traits that leaders must demonstrate in order to lead well over the long haul.
- Tithing—or the lack of it—reveals the heart condition of a leader. Tithing isn't as much about the money as it is about the heart. God expects leaders to have a right heart before Him. Business leaders, in particular, are prone to make money their god and turn it into an idol. Tithing demonstrates that the leader keeps money in its proper perspective and is willing to prioritize God before money.
- If you are bold enough to rob God or withhold from Him more than is due, you are certainly likely to do the same to employees, customers, vendors, or partners. Withholding what is rightfully owed someone else covers everything from praise, to credit for a job well done, to financial remuneration.
- Those who cheerfully tithe and plant seeds are promised blessings by God in return. In this case, a business leader who cares about his

or her people should encourage them to tithe so that they experience the rewards of obedience to God's word.

TITHING OUT OF THE TRAILER PARK

Early in our marriage, Rhonda and I were so broke that our pooled resources didn't amount to a puddle. We lived in the worst looking trailer in the trailer park and felt lucky to have it. At that time in our lives, we began to tithe in order to become more obedient to God's word. Tithing was a discipline we had long made excuses for not doing, explaining, "When we have more money, then we'll tithe. God understands our situation." In fact, the financial ramifications of giving away what little money we had made no sense at all. But from each precious paycheck, we'd give 10 percent of our gross income to the church, cutting what little corners we had left to make ends meet. Since that day, it has been quite a journey. While we've often been without abundance, we have never lacked basic necessities, and over the decades we have prospered tremendously under God's faithful hand. Looking back now, I can see how ridiculous it was to declare that God would understand our situation and that once we had more that we'd give more. The bottom line is that God doesn't understand disobedience and that tithing isn't a financial issue — it is an obedience issue that springs from a right heart. You can be sure that if your heart won't allow you to give away $100 off of $1,000, you'll never be able to part with $100,000 off of $1,000,000.

By THE BOOK Blessing

Regardless of what you say is most important to you in life, how you use your money gives you away!

WHAT DOES THE BOOK SAY ABOUT DEBT?

Next to giving money, no topic concerning biblical principles for finances creates more discomfort and reaction from business people than when I write or speak about debt. It's difficult for people in today's culture to accept that debt is wrong, but their claim that "everyone does it" doesn't make borrowing right. In fact, to declare that everyone does it is untrue. Hundreds of major corporations are debt-free. Companies as diverse as Panera Bread, American Eagle Outfitters, Gymboree, Microsoft, WebMD, Electronic Arts, and Ann Taylor are in the debt-free column, as well as droves of smaller and mid-sized enterprises.

Although THE BOOK never calls debt a sin, it is discouraged. In fact, in the Old Testament, freedom from debt was a reward for obedience, and being burdened with debt was a curse for disobedience:

> Now it shall come to pass, if you diligently obey the voice of the Lord your God, to observe carefully all His commandments which I command you today, that the Lord your God will set you high above all nations of the earth. And all these blessings shall come upon you and overtake you, because you obey the voice of the Lord your God: . . . The Lord will open to you His good treasure, the heavens, to give the rain to your land in its season, and to bless all the work of your hand. You shall lend to many nations, but you shall not borrow. (Deuteronomy 28:1–2, 12)

Now read on to discover that a curse for disobedience is being a debtor:

> But it shall come to pass, if you do not obey the voice of the Lord your God, to observe carefully all His commandments and His statutes which I command you today, that all these curses will come upon and overtake you: . . . He shall lend to you, but you shall not lend to him; he shall be the head, and you shall be the tail. (Deuteronomy 28:15, 44)

By THE BOOK Blessing

Debt traps, pressures, and restricts you like a slave. God doesn't declare debt as bad to fence you in but to free you!

Twelve Consequences of Borrowing

1. **Debt violates scripture.**[1] Paul said in his letter to the Romans: *"Owe no one anything except to love one another, for he who loves another has fulfilled the law"* (Romans 13:8). *Strong's Exhaustive Concordance of the Bible* amplifies the message behind these words: "Owe to no one, no not anything, nothing at all." Owing nothing covers more than money. Debts can include promises, possessions, meals, time, or favors.

2. **Debt produces bondage to creditors.**[2] The very nature of borrowing is entanglement. The Hebrew words for borrowing mean to entangle and twine, to take an obligation, to unite with. *"The rich rules over the poor, and the borrower is servant to the lender"* (Proverbs 22:7).

3. **Debt presumes on the future.**[3] Borrowing money doesn't show faith in God; it demonstrates an arrogant presumption! *"Come now, you who say, 'Today or tomorrow we will go to such and such a city, spend a year there, buy and sell, and make a profit; whereas you do not know what will happen tomorrow.' 'Do not boast about tomorrow, for you do not know what a day may bring forth' "*(Proverbs 27:1).

   If you begin to save money and pay cash for what you want rather than violate God's will by borrowing to obtain it, you will be far clearer on what God's desired direction is for your life. After all, if you don't have the funds available for a purchase and He doesn't provide them to you, then you can feel confident that the acquisition was not in His will or your best interests. With a pay-as-you-go financial philosophy, you live more closely under God's protection and don't rely on your own impulses or faulty wisdom. This logic applies just as well to buying a new dress as it does to acquiring one of your business competitors. Keep in mind that pride and envy are two culprits that can motivate you to go into debt for all the wrong reasons.

4. **Debt gives the illusion of independence.**[4] Borrowing gives a temporary illusion of independence from authority. It allows you to make decisions apart from God's provision of funds. In a sense, it makes you your own god, allowing you to move forward rather than wait for God's timing. This attitude is condemned by God: *"Who is he who speaks and it comes to pass, when the Lord has not commanded it?"* (Lamentations 3:37). *"For what is your life? It is even a vapor that appears for a little time and then vanishes away. Instead you ought to say, 'If the Lord wills, we shall live and do this or that.' But now you boast in your arrogance. All such boasting is evil"* (James 4:13–16).

5. **Debt evades self-examination.**[5] When God withholds funds, there is a good reason. He's sending you a signal to reevaluate your life, plans for the money, and your faith in Him. Borrowing evades these purposes and allows you to continue in your own wisdom, live in denial about where your true treasure lies, and stops you from receiving the financial blessings that come with following God's prescriptions for finances. *"Let no one deceive himself. If anyone among you seems to be wise in this age, let him become a fool that he may become wise"* (1 Corinthians 3:18).

6. **Debt interferes with God's provision.**[6] God wants to demonstrate His supernatural power through the lives of men and women of faith. Only in this way can He contrast the false confidence that people have placed in their own wisdom, abilities, and riches. Without putting yourself in a position of faith and leaving room for God to work in your finances, you may miss out on some of His greatest blessings for you. *"For the eyes of the Lord run to and fro throughout the whole earth, to show Himself strong on behalf of those whose heart is loyal to them"* (2 Chronicles 16:9).

7. **Debt removes barriers to harmful items.**[7] There are many things that you think will be beneficial to your life, but God knows that

they will be harmful to you. To protect you, He may limit your funds so that you cannot afford them. By securing the funds on your own through borrowing, you may be walking into a trap that God has tried to help you avoid: *"You ask and do not receive because you ask amiss, that you may spend it on your pleasures"* (James 4:3).

8. **Debt demonstrates discontent with the basics God has given you.**[8] God has promised to provide food and clothing. He wants you to be content with these things (1 Timothy 6:8). Borrowing is usually done for items other than these basic necessities. If money is borrowed for basic needs, it usually indicates that money that God provided for food and clothing was used for nonessentials. Coveting, and then borrowing to obtain what you covet, can cause you to lose your sense of contentment: *"Not that I speak in regard to need, for I have learned in whatever state I am, to be content: I know how to be abased, and I know how to abound"* (Philippians 4:11–12).

9. **Debt devours resources through high-interest payments.**[9] When most people borrow, they don't comprehend the final price tag of using someone else's money. Nor do they consider how, over time, interest consumes their precious resources, creating painful shortfalls of money in times of emergencies or opportunities. God expects you to be a good steward of your money and may withhold financial blessings until you are: *"He who is faithful in what is least is faithful also in much; and he who is unjust in what is least is unjust also in much. Therefore if you have not been faithful in the unrighteous mammon, who will commit to your trust the true riches?"* (Luke 16:10–11).

10. **Debt stifles resourcefulness.**[10] Christ gave two significant illustrations of men who wanted to buy expensive items. Although neither man had the money for the purchases, neither man borrowed money. Instead, they sold what they had; with the money from the sale, they bought what they wanted: *"Again, the kingdom of heaven is like treasure hidden in a field, which a man found and hid; and for joy over it he goes and sells all that he has and buys that field. Again, the kingdom of heaven is like a merchant seeking beautiful pearls, who, when he had found one pearl of great price, went and sold all that*

he had and bought it" (Matthew 13:45–46). Only when you make a firm and final decision that you will not borrow money can you be mentally, emotionally, and spiritually free to be creatively resourceful. "Easy" money is a deadening influence on creative solutions to financial needs.

11. **Debt damages God's reputation while it weakens personal faith.**[11] God has promised to provide for your needs: *"And my God shall supply all your needs according to His riches in glory by Christ Jesus"* (Philippians 4:19). When you borrow, you are saying to the world, "God is not taking care of my needs, so I will make up the difference with a loan." Debt weakens your faith, because relying on it indicates that you don't trust God during the most critical times of decision making. Just because you can afford the payment doesn't make borrowing money God's will! A clear evidence of God's will can be obtained by trusting God to provide the funds ahead of time. This is the kind of faith that pleases God. *"But without faith it is impossible to please Him . . . "* (Hebrews 11:6).

12. **Debt causes overspending and breaks sound financial discipline.**[12] Behind overspending is a basic lack of self-control that creates immense pressure on you at home and in your business, I can't count the number of business people I've seen grow their business through expansion and acquisition, creating visible signs of growth all the while their operations were poorly run. Their "growth" was a greater indicator of their credit line than their business acumen and leadership. Frankly, it was more fun to build their ego by doing deals and buying competitors than to discipline themselves to maximize the people, opportunities, and assets in their present organization. These spendthrifts routinely put their businesses on a fragile foundation in which they are one bad decision or two bad months away from insolvency. The Proverb writer warned about this sort of impulsiveness and lack of discipline: *"Also, it is not good for a soul to be without knowledge, and he sins who hastens with his feet"* (Proverbs 19:2).

By THE BOOK Blessing

When God does not provide the money, Satan tempts you to get the money in other ways. In doing so, you " . . . *fall into temptation and a snare, and into many foolish and harmful lusts, which drown men in destruction and perdition.*" (1 Timothy 6:9)

How to Make a Comeback!

Keep in mind that THE BOOK never declares that debt is a sin. Thus, God is not going to punish you as a direct result of you incurring debt. Instead, your poor decision creates the conditions whereupon you punish yourself by wasting resources, being impulsive, becoming over-extended, suffering undue stress, and incurring a potential loss of reputation and a weakened faith as you depend more on your credit line than God to provide for your needs. What happens is that, although debt is not a sin, the results of debt can cause you to behave sinfully, separating you from God and his blessings. Debt can cause you to envy, covet, resent, feel bitter, lose your peace and joy, act less lovingly, and become ill with stress. It can also cloud your vision, causing character compromises that create significant sin in your life. As you evaluate the financial crises that turn the world upside down from time to time, they're normally rooted in debt. People buy larger homes and nicer cars than they can afford, and then find they cannot afford the payments or escalating interest rates. These issues expand and create an economic domino effect that causes banks to close, businesses to close or lay off employees, and the government to initiate bailouts that create even greater debt and deficits. It can thus be justly argued that debt can be a root cause of homelessness, ruined credit, divorce, broken families, and suicide. THE BOOK's admonitions concerning debt are there to protect us and not to restrict us. God's word and wisdom will always prevail over man's ideas, trends, and philosophies.

So what do you do if you're in debt and want to become more obedient to what THE BOOK has to say about it? First, stop incurring any new debt and begin depending on God more to provide the funds you need before you need to make a purchase; if He doesn't provide the funds, then consider that He has stopped you from making a mistake. Second, begin paying down debt as you are able. This may include selling current assets and downsizing your lifestyle so that you start to develop the financial discipline that opens the doors to God's blessings on your finances. Don't feel as though you must be totally debt-free to receive new financial blessings from God, because God won't withhold his blessings until you arrive at the desired destination. Rather, He begins to bless the direction you're moving in—the journey—when you operate under His will and authority. After all, He didn't wait the 40 years it took the nation of Israel to arrive at the Promised Land to begin blessing them. He blessed and led them the whole time they were moving toward the destination—even when they stumbled, doubted, and rebelled.

What Does THE BOOK Say About Dishonest People Who Prosper?

Why do some crooks prosper? While I was conducting a conference for hundreds of pastors in Moscow, an attendee asked me, "Why does the mafia in this country live so well, while so many believers live in poverty?" My answer was "It's not your business, so don't worry about it. It's God's business, and since His ways are higher than ours, we won't always be able to understand what He allows or why He permits it." Besides, when you focus on something like this, you can lose your own sense of gratitude for what you have. I also pointed out several key Scriptures that are designed to help us be at peace with the reality that many dishonest and unscrupulous people in business—and government—prosper, while their moral counterparts live a far more basic life.

A. *"The blessing of the Lord makes one rich and He adds no sorrow to it."* (Proverbs 20:22)

This verse indicates that without the Lord's blessing behind your riches, you may have money but lack in other key areas of your life: poor physical health, unhealthy relationships, personal emptiness, strife with spouses and kids, losing what you've earned dishonestly, and the like. This is why Psalms 16:4 states: *"Their sorrows will be multiplied who hasten after another god."* In this case, the other god can be considered as chasing money or material success at any cost.

B. *"Do not fret because of evildoers, nor be envious of the wicked: For there will be no prospect for the evil man; the lamp of the wicked will be put out."* (Proverbs 24:19)

In other words, a day of reckoning will come for them. You should pity them rather than envy them. Psalms 34:9–10 assures you that God is still in control with these words: *"Oh, fear the Lord, you His saints! There is no want to those who fear Him. The young lions lack and suffer hunger. But those who seek the Lord shall not lack any good thing."*

Why do the wicked prosper while believers sometimes suffer? That's for God to know and us to find out . . . but probably not in this lifetime. For now, take solace in Jeremiah 17:9–10: *"The heart is deceitful above all things, and desperately wicked; who can know it? I, the Lord, search the heart, I test the mind, even to give every man according to his ways, according to the fruit of his doing."* Mind your own business. Keep your own heart right. Have faith in ultimate wisdom and ways of God.

By THE BOOK Blessing

As a partridge that broods but does not hatch, so is he who gets riches but not by right; it will leave him in the midst of his days, and at his end he will be a fool. (Jeremiah 17:11)

Should I Pay Taxes to a Government That Uses the Money for Immoral Purposes?

Over the centuries, citizens have used dislike of their government as reason to cheat it. In Matthew 18:22–23, Jesus has just announced to his team that He will soon be betrayed and killed. Needless to say, He had a lot on His mind. One verse later, Peter is asked by tax collectors, "Does your Teacher not pay the temple tax?" Peter answered in the affirmative and then had a short conversation with Jesus in which he was instructed to cast a hook into the sea and find a piece of money in the mouth of the first fish he caught to pay both his and Jesus' tax, so that they "not offend them." In other words, despite knowing that He would soon be killed by unjust religious leaders and their government, Jesus honored those same entities by paying them what was due.

Later, in Mathew 25, the Pharisees set out to trap Christ by asking if it was lawful to pay taxes to "Caesar," who represented the occupying force that oppressed, was feared, and was despised by the Jewish people. Suffice to say that none of the Jews present had a say in who would rule them, much less the option to vote for Candidate A over Candidate B. Yet Jesus offered the well-known reply, *"Render therefore to Caesar the things that are Caesar's, and to God the things that are God's."* In other words, if it belongs to them, give it to them. This means that you don't cheat, claim questionable deductions, hide income, or fail to file what your government requires of you.

In Romans 13, Paul instructs his followers to be subject to the governing authorities because they are appointed by God. In fact, he said that because they were appointed by God, if his hearers resisted their authority, that they also resisted the ordinance of God and would bring judgment on themselves. In verse 7, Paul states, *"Render therefore to all their due: taxes to whom taxes are due, customs to whom customs, fear to whom fear, and honor to whom honor."*

The bottom line: God expects us to pay taxes to our government, whether we like them or not, whether we voted for them or against them; He assures us that if we fail to do this, we'll bring judgment upon ourselves. Many have tried to justify cheating the government because they put the money to poor use, are immoral, and the like. But so was the government in Christ's time, yet He offered no such loopholes or excuses for failing to follow His instructions.

In fact, throughout the Scriptures you're also instructed to pray for government officials, and I can find no reprieve from this instruction if the people in power are other than those you supported. To cheat the same people you're instructed to honor and pray for would be a complete contradiction and violation of God's clear commands. Besides, when you can justify and excuse lying, cheating, or stealing to one person or group of people, what's to stop you from expanding your circle of rationalization to include clients, relatives, or employees of whom you don't approve?

Before you can ever become a leader of integrity, you must learn to follow other leaders and submit to their authority, regardless of differences. In fact, perhaps the greatest test of character comes when you disagree with legitimate authorities yet refuse to demand or justify your own way. This is a sign your heart is right, and God will honor a right heart with expanded territory for your business and increased leadership opportunities for you personally.

> Therefore submit yourselves to every ordinance of man for the Lord's sake, whether to the king as supreme, or to governors, as to those who are sent by him for the punishment of evildoers and for the praise of those who do good. For this is the will of God, that by doing good you may put to silence the ignorance of foolish men—as free, yet not using liberty as a cloak for vice, but as bondservants of God. (1 Peter 2:13–16)

By THE BOOK Blessing

Honor all people. Love the brotherhood. Fear God. Honor the king. (1 Peter 2:17)

What Does THE BOOK Say About Partners and Partnerships?

A *business partnership* can be defined as a legally binding union of two or more persons for the carrying out of business, of which they share the expenses, profits, and losses. Business partnerships differ from strategic alliances where expenses, profits, and losses are not normally shared. THE BOOK makes several clear statements concerning the dangers of business partnerships. Naturally, most partners or potential partners will argue that their special relationship and circumstances makes them an exception to these principles. For a matter of time this may appear true, but in the long run, the wisdom and warning of God's word concerning partnerships will become painfully obvious as God's word.

Four Problems with Business Partnerships

1. **Business partnerships jeopardize your reputation.**[13] In forming a business partnership, you become identified with the reputation of your partner(s). You may acquire their friends, but you'll also inherit their enemies. As your partnership continues, you'll become identified with each decision that your partner makes both on and off the job. Because you're in partnership, you do not have full control over these decisions. God blessed King Jehosophat with "*. . . riches and honor in abundance . . .*" (2 Chronicles 18:1). He had a good name. However, when he formed a partnership with wicked King Ahab, he greatly damaged his reputation. Rather than receiving riches and honor, Jehosophat received the rebuke and wrath of God. Two chapters later in 2 Chronicles 20, King Jehosophat ended his reign by allying himself with yet another wicked partner—Ahaziah, King of Israel. Verse 37 relays the bad news to Jehosophat: "*Because you have allied yourself with Ahaziah, the Lord has destroyed your works.*"

2. **Business partnerships hinder your freedom to obey God.**[14] God wants you to be free to follow scriptural direction in regard to business decisions. In a business partnership, you delegate partial

authority for these decisions to others who may not understand or appreciate scriptural financial principles. Either through their ignorance or corruption, partners who do not share your scriptural values can cause you to compromise your character and be a party to mistreating employees or customers and breaking laws. As you share in the blame for these offenses, you'll also share in the consequences. Paul warns, *"Do not be deceived: 'Evil company corrupts good habits.' Awake to righteousness, and do not sin; for some do not have the knowledge of God. I speak this to your shame"* (1 Corinthians 15:33–34).

3. **Business partnerships force you to share any chastening that God gives to your partner.**[15] God uses financial loss as a means of severely disciplining those who violate His laws. For example, an adulterer is reduced to a meager income because of God's judgment (Proverbs 6:26). A drunkard and a glutton also come to poverty (Proverbs 23:21). If your partner is openly or secretly violating God's laws, then you'll share in his or her loss when God brings discipline upon him or her.

4. **Business partnerships with nonbelievers are strongly discouraged.**[16] This is such an important point that God emphasizes it at length: *"Do not be unequally yoked together with unbelievers. For what fellowship has righteousness with lawlessness? And what communion has light with darkness? And what accord has Christ with Belial? Or what part has a believer with an unbeliever? And what agreement has the temple of God with idols? For you are the temple of the living God. As God has said: 'I will dwell in them and walk among them. I will be their God, and they shall be My people.' Therefore, 'Come out from among them and be separate,' says the Lord. 'Do not touch what is unclean, and I will receive you.'"* (2 Corinthians 6:14–17).

By THE BOOK Blessing

A good name is to be chosen rather than great riches, loving favor rather than silver and gold. (Proverbs 22:1)

SHINE THE LIGHT

You need look no further than the Book of Job to learn that riches don't insulate you from suffering. This, in itself, is reason enough to keep one's trust in God rather than in your possessions. Charles Spurgeon wrote, "A long life of prosperity may not so truly glorify God as a life checkered by adversity."[17] He added, "A man may be both good and rich, but it is not usually the case. Yet it doesn't have to be that way, for God can give people grace enough to use all their wealth to the Lord's glory."[18]

Job 42:10 tells us that after Job's trials were over, the Lord "gave him twice as much as he had before." Could it be that God knew that Job would need twice the knowledge of Him, twice the experience, twice the spiritual help, and twice the increase in wisdom before he'd be able to handle twice the wealth—and that those assets could only be brought through trials? Is it possible that Job had prayed that God would use him in a bigger way and that losing all the possessions he had, including his 10 children, was God's method for using him and bringing glory to Himself? After all, we never would have heard of Job's faithfulness and perseverance had he continued in his prosperity. The Lord intended to make him famous for his persistent faith, but as a means to that end, He first had to make him famous for suffering.[19]

As you strive to serve God and advance His kingdom, you cannot expect that He will protect you from setbacks, losses, or financial failures. If it serves His purposes to allow you to lose, He will. After all, God is glorified not so much by preserving us from trouble, as by upholding us in trouble. We wrongly assume that God will make our lives easy and remove all the obstacles in our path in return for our faithfulness to Him. But God's promises *never* imply that! Instead the promises of God express His commitment to be with us and help us when the obstacles are greatest. It is only in facing, and living through, pain and tragedy that we experience God's faithfulness.

You may tithe, stay out of debt, avoid unwise business partnerships, and still suffer financial reversals. Don't despair; God is at work and in control. The key is to remain obedient and totally dependent upon God's wisdom and not to take matters into your hands and attempt to turn things around in your own power. Your obedience through trials and tests will promote the trust and growth that makes you even more blessable after God has taught you what He wants you to know and used your travails for His benefit.

Trials are your education for the future. All too often, God's children are unprepared to enjoy greater success until they've suffered the humility of defeat. If you haven't suffered financial setbacks for a while, but want to grow both spiritually and financially, then it may be wise to consider that your heart may not be ready to move on to more success and greater wealth until it has been enlarged by God through trials and tests. When you traverse tough times with this perspective they become not only more bearable, but exciting.

Summary

All four financial matters discussed in this chapter—tithing, shunning debt, not concerning yourself with prosperity of dishonest people, and avoiding business partnerships—require discipline and faith. The blessings for obeying these biblical concepts are clearly outlined in THE BOOK, as are the consequences for disobedience. Wherever you're at in your financial life is the result of choices you've made in the past. To get to a better place in the future you must begin making better choices now. You cannot violate God's clearly stated principles concerning money and expect to escape the consequences. At the same time, right choices open the door to financial blessings you could never expect to attain through your own wisdom or efforts. God's laws concerning money are clear. You don't have to understand them—you just need to obey them!

Revelation

How do you keep perspective when an economic upheaval can cause your business, savings, home value, investments, and retirement nest egg to shrink and, in some cases, disappear altogether? Habakkuk, a

175

contemporary of Jeremiah and Ezekiel whom God commissioned to lead in troubled times around 622 B.C., had this wisdom to share with us:

> Even though the fig trees have no blossoms, and there are no grapes on the vines; even though the olive crop fails, and the fields lie empty and barren; even though the flocks die in the fields, and the cattle barns are empty, yet I will rejoice in the Lord! I will be joyful in the God of my salvation! (Habakkuk 3:17–18)

Habakkuk knew what to do when things seemed completely hopeless. His world was literally falling apart around him. There was destruction everywhere he looked. But Habakkuk knew that God was bigger than his circumstances! So what did he do? He invited God into his circumstances by rejoicing and praising the Lord. He made the choice to be joyful, knowing that it would connect him to the One who would deliver him! If you truly believe Romans 8:28—that *"all things work together for good to those who love God and are called according to His purpose"*—then you should consider using current financial struggles or setbacks to your advantage in the following ways:

- Shift your trust away from your "stuff" and back to God as your true Source of security, peace, provision, and wisdom.
- Take the opportunity to continue to show faithfulness when you tithe, even though financial pressures make it seem less feasible.
- Refuse to blame God by recalling the words and eventual victory of Job: *"Naked I came from my mother's womb, and naked I shall return there. The Lord gave, and the Lord has taken away; Blessed be the name of the Lord"* (Job 1:21–22). In all this Job did not sin nor charge God with wrong.

ACTION EXERCISE

STRATEGIES FOR MANAGING PERSONAL AND BUSINESS FINANCES

Review the four principles and points concerning money, and list the three that are your highest value takeaways from each section:

1. _____
2. _____
3. _____
4. _____

CHAPTER 8

Four Steps to Build Your Team by THE BOOK

Genesis

When I was promoted from salesperson to manager, I had no idea how to build a team. In fact, I thought that if we all showed up at work together at the same time and place for a number of weeks or months that a team would automatically develop. Not quite! Rather, I found that sometimes a gang or a band of mercenaries would develop, rather than a team, and that great teams were built with intent and not by chance.

You cannot expect to build a great team unless you start with the right people. For years, I hired the wrong folks and tried to teach them to be talented and driven. I learned later that you have to hire people who bring something to the table and who give you something to work with. I made the mistake of failing to set clear vision, values, and performance expectations and then becoming frustrated when my team wouldn't do what I expected of them. I was also under the notion that I had an obligation to spend equal time, energy, and resources among all team members and many times discovered that I spent inordinate amounts of time with bottom dwellers in an attempt to elevate them up to becoming at least average, ignoring my best performers in the process. Accountability was another of my weaknesses, primarily because I never set clear standards to hold the team accountable for in the first place. Perhaps my biggest mistake was making my people so dependent upon me that they were worthless when I wasn't around. I micromanaged them to an extent that they couldn't think for themselves, wouldn't make decisions, and never initiated change or took risks.

I learned the hard way that my "lousy" team was a reflection of my own inept leadership skills and that if I wanted to improve the people around me, I would need to start personally doing more of the right things. In this chapter I'll cover four key points to building an effective team. Fortunately, THE BOOK provides a solid framework for making this happen so that you do not have to experiment with trial and error or trust in your own wisdom. The chances are excellent that you're already doing many of these steps well. Some are commonsense strategies that leaders figure out intuitively. Other actions are more unconventional and will require that you keep an open mind and follow THE BOOK's model rather than what you may have been force-fed by business professors, bosses, or books based on man's thoughts and ways. I can promise you that whether you lead 1 or 1,000, these four strategies will work if you're diligent in executing them consistently.

The biggest challenge in that last sentence is the word "consistently." Too many leaders follow the "rebellion, repression, repentance, restoration" cycle in their business. In other words, when things are going well they begin to rebel against the godly principles that brought them to success in the first place and do things more according to what is wise or convenient in their own eyes. These actions bring about repression, which always follows rebellion. Repression is when you begin to reap the consequences of your poor choices and lose momentum, morale, and credibility and suffer loss both personally and as an organization. Your self-inflicted hardships bring about repentance—when you turn away from your own methods and return to God, focusing on what is truly important and purifying your motives as a leader. At this stage your team checks egos, cuts budgets, downsizes, regroups, and refocuses. The result of repentance brings about restoration—when you regain the favor and blessings that come with operating under God's word and enjoy the blessings of obedience. All this is to say: Don't fall into the rebellion stage once you get successful! Execute these principles day-in and day-out, without compromise or excuse!

HIRE SLOWLY AND STRATEGICALLY

Hiring recklessly is one of the most costly mistakes in business. You cannot calculate the cost of hiring just one wrong person for your team. You may be able to quantify the loss of production a low performer costs you, but the lower momentum, morale, and diminished credibility that results from a bad hire is incalculable.

Three Tips to Hiring Right

1. **Pray before making a hiring decision.** As basic as the principle is, most leaders I ask admit to never doing this! Pray that God sends you the right people and that He gives you wisdom and discernment during the interview. If Jesus prayed before selecting His team, so should you!

   > Now it came to pass in those days that He went out to the mountain to pray, and continued all night in prayer to God. And when it was day, He called His disciples to Himself. (Luke 6:12)

2. **Hire those who are already working and productive.** One of the chief complaints I hear at my seminars is that "there is a shortage of talented people in my marketplace." This is untrue. There is no shortage of talented people in a given area. It is unlikely that the Creator got ticked off at your city and stopped putting talented people there! What is more likely is that the most productive, successful, and effective people in your marketplace already have jobs! Thus, you must change your strategy to focus more on

attracting qualified, passive job candidates into your business rather than expecting to build a team of eagles from among the ranks of the unemployed! The disciples whom Jesus called were busy, working people. In fact, He hunted them rather than posting an ad and then sitting back and waiting to be hunted. Jesus recruited an employed Matthew:

> As Jesus passed on from there, He saw a man named Matthew sitting at the tax office. And He said to him, "Follow Me." So he arose and followed Him. (Matthew 5:9)

Jesus recruited employed fishermen who had worked all night:

> So it was, as the multitude pressed about Him to hear the word of God, that He stood by the Lake of Gennesaret, and saw two boats standing by the lake; but the fishermen had gone from them and were washing their nets. Then He got into one of the boats, which was Simon's, and asked him to put out a little from the land. And He sat down and taught the multitudes from the boat.
>
> When He stopped speaking, He said to Simon, "Launch out into the deep and let down your nets for a catch."
>
> But Simon answered and said to Him, "Master, we have toiled all night and caught nothing; nevertheless at Your word I will let down the net." And when they had done this, they caught a great number of fish, and their net was breaking. So they signaled to their partners in the other boat to come and help them. And they came and filled both the boats, so that they began to sink. When Simon Peter saw it, he fell down at Jesus' knees, saying, "Depart from me, for I am a sinful man, O Lord!"
>
> For he and all who were with him were astonished at the catch of fish which they had taken; and so also were

James and John, the sons of Zebedee, who were partners with Simon. And Jesus said to Simon, "Do not be afraid. From now on you will catch men." So when they had brought their boats to land, they forsook all and followed Him. (Luke 5:1–11)

3. **Hire people who give you something to work with.** You can teach skills and knowledge but you cannot teach talent, character, drive, attitude, or energy. You must hire these five traits into your organization. How do you know if someone has them? While you may never know with absolute certainty, you can improve your odds by digging deep into their track record during an interview and into their lives as these five traits — or the lack of them — will show up in someone's life.

The verse in James 1:17 shows that talent is a gift from God. You cannot teach it! As a leader, you must draw out of someone what was inside of them; you cannot put inside of them what was left out!

Every good gift and every perfect gift is from above and comes down from the Father of lights, with whom there is no variation or shadow of turning. (James 1:17)

The words in Acts 16:3 show the importance of the good reputation and track record of Timothy:

He [Timothy] was well spoken of by the brethren who were at Lystra and Iconium. Paul wanted to have him go on with him. (Acts 16:3)

Acts 18:26 gives an example of the character-based teachable spirit of Apollos, who had great oratory skill but lacked sound doctrine. He responded well to his correction and was used mightily in ministry:

So he [Apollos] began to speak boldly in the synagogue. When Aquila and Priscilla heard him, they took him

aside and explained to him the way of God more accu-
rately. (Acts 18:26)

One of the most helpful lessons I've learned in training and coaching
people over the years is this: I can help you become more than you are,
but I cannot make you something that you are not. In other words, if you
give me something to work with, I can help you nurture those gifts and
convert your potential into results. However, if you don't have drive, I
cannot make you driven. If you don't have energy, I cannot make you
energized. If you have weak character, I cannot make you a person of
integrity. If you have no talent for the job at hand, I cannot make you
talented for that position. And if you have a poor attitude, I can alter
your mood from time to time, but I cannot make you have a positive
outlook on life. Knowing what I can and cannot control about someone's
behavior and performance frees me to invest in those who have the right
stuff and to cut my losses with those who do not.

By THE BOOK Lesson in Leadership

Heart Trumps Appearance or Personality!

One of the biggest mistakes in hiring is when you make an emotional
decision during an interview that you either like or dislike the person based
on his or her appearance or personality, or your own biases, prejudices, or
stereotypes. Normally, you make an emotional decision early on in an
interview and you begin to lose your objectivity as to whether or not the
person is the best candidate to perform the work you need done. When
you like someone too quickly, you stop assessing him or her and start
selling the job, losing all leverage in the process! When you don't like him
or her, you grow bored and want them out of your office so that you can go
on to what is next. However, THE BOOK offers wisdom into the fallacy of
making emotional decisions as found in 1 Samuel. In this chapter, Samuel
is evaluating all eight of Jesse's children, in search for whom God wants
him to anoint as the future king of Israel:

> So it was, when they came, that he [Samuel] looked at Eliab and said, "Surely the Lord's anointed is before Him."
>
> But the Lord said to Samuel, "Do not look at his appearance or at his physical stature, because I have refused him. For the Lord does not see as man sees; for man looks at the outside appearance, but the Lord looks at the heart." (1 Samuel 16:6–7)

After refusing the first seven of Jesse's sons, Samuel discovered and anointed David—the youngest son who was so insignificant he was out tending sheep while "King Search" was taking place with his seven brothers. Incidentally, when Goliath taunted the Israeli army for 40 straight days, challenging any of the soldiers to fight him, three of David's elder brothers, including the "kingly looking" Eliab, were among the ranks of the Israelis who were too fearful to fight.

The Book of John tells an oft-overlooked story concerning Jesus' criteria for recruiting others:

> The following day Jesus wanted to go to Galilee, and He found Phillip and said to him, "Follow Me." Now Phillip was from Bethsaida, the city of Andrew and Peter. Phillip found Nathanael and said to him, "We have found Him of whom Moses in the law, and also the prophets wrote—Jesus of Nazareth, the son of Joseph."
>
> And Nathanael said to him, "Can anything good come out of Nazareth?"
>
> Phillip said to him, "Come and see."
>
> Jesus saw Nathanael coming toward Him, and said of him, "Behold, an Israelite in whom is no deceit!"
>
> Nathanael said to Him, "How do You know me?"
>
> Jesus answered and said to him, "Before Phillip called you, when you were under the fig tree, I saw you."
>
> Nathanael answered and said to Him, "Rabbi, You are the Son of God! You are the King of Israel!"
>
> Jesus answered and said to him, "Because I said to you, 'I saw you under the fig tree,' do you believe? You will see greater things than these." (John 1:43–50)

So what did Jesus see in Nathanael? First, if Jesus could see him under the fig tree, He also undoubtedly knew of his remark to Phillip, *"Can anything good come out of Nazareth?"* Those words indicate that Nathanael was an honest skeptic, someone who would think for himself and would not be an unthinking sheep, blindly following the herd. Second, when Jesus saw him, he detected his character as evidenced by his words, *"Behold, an Israelite indeed, in whom is no deceit!"* Jesus saw that Nathanael was an honest man, with a character free of deception. Third, Jesus referred to seeing Nathanael under a fig tree. In biblical times, a fig tree, because of its shade, was a common place for men of prayer to go and pray. The fig tree was a prayer closet of sorts, and it is probably safe to assume that Jesus was more likely to single out seeing Nathanael there—after all, He could have seen him anywhere—because Nathanael was praying and not because he was catching a nap. Any leader wanting to run his or her business by THE BOOK should value these same three key traits in those they bring on to their team: (a) an honest skeptic who thinks for him or herself, (b) strong character with no deceit, and (c) a person of prayer.

By THE BOOK Blessing

Do not judge according to appearance, but judge with righteous judgment. (John 7:24)

DEFINE REALITY IN YOUR ORGANIZATION

It does little good to hire great people and then fail to create reality for them within your organization. Reality is made up of three components: vision, values, and performance expectations. These three components define direction, boundaries, and criteria for measuring performance, making decisions, and solving problems. They also establish a benchmark for accountability. There are many things you can delegate as a leader but defining reality in your organization is not one of them. You're expected to see farther, more, and sooner than your followers. Reality in your organization is not something that you vote on. Although it is wise to gain input from others concerning these issues, as a leader it is ultimately your responsibility to determine vision, values, and performance expectations for your organization.

The Three Aspects of Reality

1. **Vision. This defines direction in a clear, measurable manner.** In the Book of Nehemiah, Nehemiah cast a bold and compelling vision for the nation of Israel to rebuild the Jerusalem Wall that had been in ruins for 123 years. His vision united the people, gave them a common purpose, and inspired them to work diligently until completion and resulted in an astounding success: The Jerusalem Wall was rebuilt in 52 days! Nehemiah's vision call was simple and to the point:

   > Come and let us build the wall of Jerusalem, that we
   > may no longer be a reproach. (Nehemiah 1:17)

   What is the vision for your organization? Is it measurable? Does it influence the daily behaviors and performances of your people? If not, then it is impotent. To know if your vision is real, all you must do is pass out 10 index cards to 10 different employees and ask them to write the vision for your organization without conferring with one another. If all the answers are identical when you gather the cards—congratulations! If they're not, you have work to do because you've lost your vision and, as a result, your people are probably unconsciously working against one another rather than toward a common end.

2. **Core Values. These are the behaviors you've decided you're unwilling to compromise on.** Oftentimes leaders have established performance expectations for their enterprises—the quantifiable performance numbers that must be hit—but they fail to establish clear behavioral expectations. Unfortunately, this can give employees

187

the notion that their behaviors aren't relevant as long as they hit their numbers. To be fair, some leaders take the right first step and establish core values, but they never live them personally or hold others accountable for doing the same. They frame the values on parchment and hang them in the hallway with much fanfare for all to see, but without the ability to positively influence behaviors on a daily basis, the values are relegated to little more than décor.

Leaders throughout the Old and New Testaments established behavioral expectations, repeated them often, and held others accountable for their embodiment. Perhaps the most well-known occasion of values-casting was when Christ gave His Sermon on the Mount and offered what has become known as the Beatitudes. You can read His complete list of behavioral expectations, many of which rocked the world of those who heard them, in the fifth chapter of Matthew. After declaring the values, He did something even more important: He brought them to life by living them. Following His example in this regard is essential if you expect the values you establish to become alive and shape your culture rather than amount to a laughable experiment in wishful thinking.

Two sample values from THE BOOK:

> You shall not take vengeance, nor bear any grudge against the children of your people, but you shall love your neighbor as yourself. (Leviticus 19:8)
>
> Love your enemies, bless those who curse you, do good to those who hate you, and pray for those who spitefully use you and persecute you. (Matthew 5:44)

3. **Performance Expectations.** These are the specific outputs you have outlined as non-negotiable — "the numbers." They may include metrics ranging from a number of sales, a certain number of appointments set, a specific quantity of presentations given, a total amount of gross revenue worth of products or services sold, and the like.

188

Jesus gave a bold performance expectation to His disciples, and it is one that all of His followers will someday be measured against. They are His last recorded words in the Gospel of Matthew:

> Go therefore and make disciples of all nations, baptizing them in the name of the Father and of the Son and of the Holy Spirit, teaching them to observe all things that I have commanded you; and lo, I am with you always, even to the end of the age. (Matthew 28:19)

THE VALUE OF VALUES AND PERFORMANCE EXPECTATIONS

Establishing core values and performance expectations accomplishes several key leadership objectives:

- It helps define reality in your organization.
- It establishes a benchmark for accountability.
- It removes gray areas and takes away the excuse of ignorance that people can and will claim if what you expect is cloudy: "I didn't know that was what you wanted," "You should have been clearer," or "I can't read your mind. It's not my fault that it didn't work out."
- It makes it easier for you to make decisions. After all, if someone is not hitting the numbers or living the values, the fact that you must either quickly turnaround or terminate the employee is a simple call. It's always easier to make decisions if you've established up front what you stand for.

A SLIP OF THE HEAD OR A FAULT FROM THE HEART?

You may be familiar with my book *If You Don't Make Waves You'll Drown* (John Wiley & Sons, 2005). In Chapter 1, page 29, there is a list of 25 sample behavioral expectations called "The Business Facts of Life." One of these expectations states, "If you lie, cheat, or steal, I will fire you. There will be no second warning." This particular expectation happens to be one of the behavioral expectations in our company. I simply will not tolerate any degree of lying, cheating, or stealing—period.

Recently, we had to hold accountable an employee who lied concerning his actions. Some will say, "You fired him for a mistake? Why didn't you forgive him and give him a second chance?" My reasoning may help you to deal with similar situations. Although you may or may not agree with the course we took to enforce our values, you should consider the difference between an employee who makes a mistake from the head versus one who deliberately sins from the heart. You should also consider the resulting implications for you, your customers, and other team members.

First, a lie is more than a mistake. A typo is a mistake; turning in the wrong paperwork is a mistake; forgetting to call someone when you said that you would is a mistake. On the other hand, a lie is a deliberate and willful act of dishonesty. It springs from the heart and cannot be written off as a mere slip of the head. In fact, it reflects the condition of one's heart, which portends continuing character issues with the same employee in the future. Two particular verses in Proverbs explain why heart issues should be taken very seriously:

> Keep your heart with all diligence, for out of it spring the issues of life. (Proverbs 4:23)
>
> For as he thinks in his heart, so is he. "Eat and drink!" he says to you, but his heart is not with you. (Proverbs 23:7)

As for forgiveness, we absolutely forgave the employee who lied. However, we still fired him. Forgiveness doesn't mean freedom from consequences. It means that you release any bitterness or resentment you have toward someone and no longer hold what they did against him or her. We wish this young man the best. But I will not subject my customers or employees to his future faults from the heart. I can help someone correct mistakes from the head with training and coaching. But a heart issue is not something I can greatly impact. This employee's heart condition was further revealed when he never apologized or expressed remorse for having lied, choosing instead to leave the building in a huff.

During the confrontation with his supervisor, he lied twice in two minutes despite being cautioned, "I'm going to ask you a question and I need the truth. If you lie to me, you're finished here." If he had told the truth, he would still have a job.

It is also important to understand that the terminated employee was well aware of this particular value. He had read the book, heard me discuss its application, and had seen each Business Fact of Life filmed and placed onto video as I produced them. He was not in a gray area. He understood what was expected, as well as the consequences for falling short.

When your employees violate expectations, it's important to look at the root cause: head problem or heart problem? This diagnosis will help you better decide the course you should take. What is most important is that you realize that issues of the heart cannot be remedied by you, as the offending employee's leader. You can admonish someone, pray for the person, direct them to spiritual truths concerning their behavior, and more. But, ultimately, they must repent and seek reconciliation with God. This fact limits both your options concerning the current situation as well as the influence you have over their future behavior. It is because of these reasons that we have so little tolerance for those who violate our values and find it easier, rather than more difficult, to make the tough choices concerning consequences for those who abuse them. Because we took the action that we did, you are also safe in assuming that everyone in our organization believes that our core values are for real.

One of the most significant benefits of having clear behavioral and performance expectations is that the wrong people will fire themselves. This helps protect you from one of a leader's most common faults, which is to keep the wrong person too long.

By THE BOOK Blessing

If you know these things, blessed are you if you do them. (John 13:17)

ESTABLISH A HIGH-ACCOUNTABILITY CULTURE

Because ambiguity is the enemy of accountability, you'll be unsuccessful establishing a high-accountability culture until you first define reality as outlined in the previous section. While defining reality is the first component of a high-accountability culture, it is not the final word. You also need fast, honest feedback on performance and consequences for failing to perform. Fast, honest feedback eliminates gray areas and gives you a chance to reinforce productive behaviors, while quickly confronting those behaviors that are counterproductive. Consequences are the "or else" that must be attached to wrong behaviors and results. Without the consequence, you are unlikely to change a wrong behavior. Failing to provide a consequence for detrimental behaviors actually reinforces the bad behavior, guaranteeing that you will see more of it in the future.

DEVELOP A LOW THRESHOLD FOR EXCUSES!

In a business climate where there is increasingly less margin for error, it is important to strengthen your high-accountability culture by developing a low threshold for the excuses people use to explain away their lack of success. Oftentimes, these employees are able to generate results when favorable economic conditions prevail, but when the economy's momentum reverses, their deficient abilities are exposed and they resort to excuses for failing to perform.

Following are four fast facts about excuses to create a stronger perspective on their cost to your organization. For these same reasons, it is important that as a leader you also refrain from making excuses and focus instead on solutions.

Four Fast Facts About Excuses

1. **Excuses are the natural assassin of progress.** If you're focused on reasons why something didn't get done or can't be done, you're simply not available to focus on the consistent and right actions that would bring progress and success.

2. **Excuses are a distraction and a diversion.** Excuses distract by focusing on apparent problems rather than solutions, and they divert valuable time, energy, and resources from productive activities to defensive, counterproductive non-action.

3. **Excuses are the DNA of underachievers.** Excuses label you as weak; as one who refuses to take responsibility; as one who blames; as one who is common, ordinary, and run-of-the-mill.

4. **One of the best days of your life is the day you renounce excuses.** Giving up excuses is liberating and marks the day of your life when you finally grow up. It frees your talents, focus, and energy to invest in what is productive. It also is the day you give yourself permission to fail, admit it, and learn from your actions . . . which makes you far more valuable in the workplace.

By THE BOOK Blessing

Jesus said, "Do you want to be made well?" The sick man answered Him, "Sir, I have no man to put me into the pool when the water is stirred up; but while I am coming, another steps down before me." Jesus said to him, "Rise, take up your bed and walk." (John 5:6–8)

BY THE BOOK LESSON IN LEADERSHIP

CARE ENOUGH TO CONFRONT!

As a leader, you must care enough about your people to confront them when they are wrong, off track, or engaging in destructive behavior. As I pointed out in Chapter 1, caring enough to confront doesn't mean that you need to shout, get personal, or be sarcastic. It simply mandates that you are firm, direct, and clear.

In Matthew 16:21, we find Jesus sharing the news of His impending death with His disciples:

> From that time Jesus began to show to His disciples that He must go to Jerusalem, and suffer many things from the elders and chief priests and scribes, and be killed, and be raised on the third day.
>
> Then Peter took Him aside and began to rebuke Him saying: "Far be it from You, Lord; this shall not happen to You!"
>
> But He turned and said to Peter, "Get behind Me, Satan! You are an offense to Me, for you are not mindful of the things of God, but the things of men." (Matthew 16:21–23)

Jesus had to set Peter straight in no uncertain terms and get his thinking back on the team's ultimate mission rather than what might be uncomfortable for him to fathom at the moment. He specifically, clearly, and firmly pointed out Peter's faulty reasoning and shortsighted thinking. But what He did next is also a key lesson in accountability and should always follow the confrontation conversation: He established a performance expectation.

> Then Jesus said to His disciples, "If anyone desires to come after Me, let him deny himself, and take up his cross and follow Me. For whoever desires to save his life will lose it, but whoever loses his life for My sake will find it." (Matthew 16:24–25)

The follow-up after the confrontation is a pattern that must be followed when you address errant behavior or performance from employees. Yes, you should care enough about them to confront them, but don't leave them there. Explain or redefine what is expected, along with potential payoffs for success or penalties for falling short.

It would have been difficult for anyone ever encountering Christ in person to accuse Him of letting them live in a gray area. Jesus let you know where you stood, even if you didn't want to hear it. But He confronted in love. He may have detested the performance but He still loved the performer.

WHEN IS ENOUGH, ENOUGH?

A question that often arises concerning confrontations is "How many chances or warnings should I give someone?" Naturally, it depends upon the offense. Personally, I don't believe that thieves should be given multiple chances to pilfer your organization before letting them go. But how about attitude issues or other defective behaviors? Two Scriptures give us some insight here:

> Reject a divisive man after the first and second admonition, knowing that such a person is warped and sinning, being self-condemned. (Titus 3:10)
>
> So the Lord God became angry with Solomon, because his heart had turned from the Lord God of Israel, who had appeared to him twice, and had commanded him concerning this thing, that he should not go after other gods; but he did not keep what the Lord had commanded. Therefore the Lord said to Solomon, "Because you have done this, and have not kept My covenant and My statutes, which I have commanded you, I will surely tear the kingdom away from you and give it to your servant." (1 Kings 11:9–11)

THE BOOK also offers instruction for how a younger person should confront one who is older, younger, or a peer. *"Do not rebuke an older man, but exhort him as a father, younger men as brothers, older women as mothers, younger women as sisters, with all purity."* (Timothy 5:11)

By THE BOOK Lesson in Leadership

The Consequence Should Fit the Crime and the Time

THE BOOK offers numerous examples of consequences for wrong behavior. Perhaps one of the most dramatic is found in the Book of Acts when the new church is just getting started and a man and his wife decide to lie and deceive fellow believers. They had just sold some land and made a big deal about bringing the proceeds to the apostles to distribute to the poor. No one forced them to sell their house, and they were free to keep whatever proceeds that they wanted. The problem with their behavior arose when they conspired to lie to the apostles, to the Holy Spirit, and to the other believers about the true amount they sold it for to give the impression that they were donating 100 percent of the proceeds, when they had actually conspired to keep some for themselves. The acts of making false impressions and lying to promote oneself in the eyes of others ran counter to the values represented by the new church. Perhaps the drastic consequence Ananias and Saphhira suffered is to remind us that there are times when the stakes are higher and there is less margin for error, and during those times the consequences for wrong behavior must be swift and severe. This was one of those times. As the new church was in its infancy the credibility of its values and mission was at stake. Thus, read this story in that context to better understand why the consequence in this instance not only had to fit the crime but the timing of the offense.

Acts 5:1–12: Set the stage: The church had just agreed in Acts 4 that the members would sell their belongings and distribute to each as anyone needed. The values of the new church had just been established and followers were sure to notice whether or not the values were for real or mere suggestions.

> But a certain man named Ananias, with Saphhira, his wife, sold a possession. And he kept back part of the proceeds, his wife also being aware of it, and brought a certain part and laid it by the apostle's feet. But Peter said, "Ananias, why has Satan filled your heart to lie to the Holy Spirit and keep back part of the price of land for yourself? While it remained, was it not your own? And after it was sold, was it not in your own control? Why have you conceived this thing in your heart? You have not lied to men, but to God." And Ananias, hearing these words, fell down and breathed his last. So great fear came upon all who heard these things. And the young men wrapped him up, carried him out, and buried him.
>
> Now it was about three hours later when his wife came in, not knowing what had happened. And Peter answered her, "Tell me whether you sold the land for this much."
>
> She said, "Yes, for so much."

Then Peter said to her, "How is it that you have agreed together to test the Spirit of the Lord? Look, the feet of those who have buried your husband are at the door, and they will carry you out." Then immediately, she fell down at his feet and breathed her last. And the young men came in and found her dead, and carrying her out, buried her by her husband. So great fear came upon all the church and upon all who heard these things (Acts 5:1–12).

There is no more important time to act with urgency in enforcing vision, values, and performance expectations than soon after they're enacted. Whenever a new program, movement, or initiative is in its infancy, its credibility and sustainability are up for grabs. The integrity of the entire enterprise rides on your ability and willingness to act quickly and decisively to protect the legitimacy of your standards, the team, and the organization. And this means that the personal comfort level of any one individual must become subordinate to the greater good of your team and mission.

By THE BOOK Blessing

Moreover, if your brother sins against you, go and tell him his fault between you and him alone. If he hears you, you have gained your brother. (Matthew 18:15)

DEVELOP AN INNER CIRCLE

Perhaps the greatest lesson I learned from THE BOOK concerning building a team is that you must spend greater amounts of time with smaller numbers of strategic people mentoring, sharing, and reproducing yourself into their lives. This "smaller number of strategic people" is your inner circle. Every effective leader needs to build an inner circle that helps him or her carry the load because there is only so

197

much any one person can accomplish on his or her own. Your inner circle is the person or people in whom you see the highest upward potential for growth. Normally, leaders spend little time with this group as they take them for granted and invest inordinate amounts of time with poor performers trying to pull them up to a level of acceptability. However, if you hire slowly and strategically, define clear standards for performance and behaviors, and hold people accountable for results, you should not have bottom dwellers who continually drain your time, energy, and resources. Because of this, you'll be able to pour yourself into your inner circle and equip them to operate at a higher level of performance and rapidly advance the growth of your organization in the process.

Too many leaders are under the politically correct illusion that they must spend the same amount of time with everyone and divide organizational resources and opportunities equitably among all team members. Nothing could be further from the truth or more detrimental to the growth of your organization.

Three Steps to Develop Your Inner Circle

1. **Identify and invest more into those in your organization with the highest upward potential.** They must be ready, willing, and able to grow.

   Once you identify these people, customize a growth program with them to help close the gap between where they are currently in their level of abilities and what you see as their "next level" of contribution to your organization. This means that you will spend more time personally with the fewer number of people in whom you see the highest potential for growth.

   Jesus was the ultimate example of how this process works. Jesus cared about and loved all of His team. But He did not spend equal time with them! Following are three examples of "spending greater amounts of time with smaller numbers of strategic people," as well as a sample from Moses, who mentored Joshua, and Paul, who mentored Timothy.

198

As soon as Jesus heard the word that was spoken, He said to the ruler of the synagogue, "Do not be afraid; only believe." And He permitted no one to follow Him except Peter, James and John, the brother of James. (Mark 5:36)

Now it came to pass, about eight days after these sayings, that He took Peter, John and James and went up on the mountain to pray. As He prayed, the appearance of His face was altered, and His robe became white and glistening. (Luke 9:28)

Then they came to a place which was named Gethsemane; and He said to His disciples, "Sit here while I pray." And He took Peter, James and John with Him, and He began to be troubled and deeply distressed. Then He said to them, "My soul is exceedingly sorrowful, even to death. Stay here and watch." (Mark 14:32)

Now Joshua the son of Nun was full of the spirit of wisdom, for Moses had laid his hands on him. (Deuteronomy 34:9)

Joshua was Moses' protégé and picked up where his mentor left off. He led the Israelites into the Promised Land, defeated the enemies who stood in their way, and lived to see God's people established in the land that was promised to them hundreds of years before. Unfortunately, Joshua failed to follow Moses' example and mentored no one to take his place. As a result, Israel languished for hundreds of erratic years under a series of 12 judges before a monarchy was established.

O Timothy! Guard what was committed to your trust, avoiding the profane and idle babblings and contradictions of what is falsely called knowledge—by professing it some have strayed concerning the faith. (1 Timothy 6:20–21)

Paul was an incredible mentor to Timothy. In fact, the Book of 1 Timothy is a leadership manual that should be required reading for all leaders.

THE BOOK is filled with other outstanding examples of mentoring relationships that are worthy of your study. As you read THE BOOK, look for the mentorship lessons between Abraham and Lot, Jethro and Moses, Deborah and Barak, Naomi and Ruth, Mordecai and Esther, Eli and Samuel, David and Solomon, Elijah and Elisha, Barnabas and Saul, Barnabas and John Mark, Paul and Titus, among many others.

2. **Give up power so that you can go up higher!** You will never build an inner circle if you continue to do too much of the work by yourself! The measure of your leadership is not how much you can do personally but how much you can get done through others. Remember that perhaps the greatest leadership lesson of all time is that you can't do it alone!

Following are three well-known Scriptures that demonstrate this principle:

> And when He had called His twelve disciples to Him, He
> gave them power over unclean spirits, to cast them out,
> and to heal all kinds of sickness and all kinds of disease.
> (Matthew 10:1–2)

The next verse from Ephesians reminds you that it is your job to equip others to do more work and not to try and do it all by yourself:

> And He gave some to be apostles, some prophets, some
> evangelists, and some pastors and teachers, for *the equip-
> ping* (author's emphasis): of the saints for the work of the
> ministry, for the edifying of the body of Christ. . . .
> (Ephesians 4:11–12)

The following Scriptures from Acts point to a pivotal moment in the growing church when the 12 disciples realized that they were doing too much by themselves and needed to focus more on priorities. As a result, they empowered qualified members of their team to operate at a more significant level of service. Although I presented these scriptures in Chapter 2 as examples of time management and putting first things first, they are just as relevant when covering the topic of giving up power to go up higher!

> Then the twelve summoned the multitude of the disciples and said, "It is not desirable that we should leave the word of God and serve tables. Therefore, brethren, seek out from you seven men of good reputation, full of the Holy Spirit and wisdom, whom we may appoint over this business; but we will give ourselves continually to prayer and to the ministry of the word." (Acts 6:2–4)

3. **Hold your inner circle accountable for results.** Oftentimes you can be wrong about who should be in your inner circle. You see potential and talent in someone and work hard to draw it out but never realize the results that you should. Without a doubt, potential and talent, although important, are two of the most overrated qualities in man. The bottom line is that talent doesn't make you special, nor does potential. After all, unrealized talent and potential are pervasive in any organization. What is special is when someone is able to convert their potential and talent into results! This is why it is acceptable to work with someone according to their potential for a period of time, but ultimately you must measure them by their actual performance in order to determine the depth of your future investment in them. As the following scripture from Mark reminds us, if you've been given a lot, a lot will be expected of you in return.

> Take heed what you hear. With the same measure you use, it will be measured to you; and to you who hear, more will be given. For whoever has, to him more will be given; but whoever does not have, even what he has will be taken away from him. (Mark 4:24)

One mistake that owners or CEOs of companies make is that they give too much benefit of the doubt to poor leaders. They give an unproductive manager more time to show results than they do a less productive subordinate. This is opposite of what it should be! Ineffective managers should be given less time and less rope, because when they eventually hang themselves, they tend to take a lot of other people with them.

Jesus' reaction toward the unproductive fig tree should remind us that we also need to expect fruit from those we've entrusted with fruitbearing. And when the tree — the organization — isn't producing the fruit, or produces bad fruit, you don't cut off or blame the branches — the subordinates — but you must examine the roots — the managers — and hold them accountable.

> Now in the morning, As He returned to the city He was hungry. And seeing a fig tree by the road, He came to it and found nothing on it but leaves, and said to it, "Let no fruit grow on you ever again." Immediately, the fig tree withered and died. (Matthew 21:18)

SHINE THE LIGHT

Many leaders fail to develop others to their fullest potential because their leadership style more resembles a cop than a coach. Yet as strange as it may seem, cops and coaches have several things in common:

1. Both cops and coaches have authority.
2. Both cops and coaches enforce guidelines and behavioral boundaries.
3. Both cops and coaches will give feedback on performance. This feedback is normally given quickly after the behavior and is most often direct and firm in its nature.
4. Both cops and coaches hold others accountable for results.
5. Both cops and coaches apply consequences for behavioral defects.

Despite these commonalities, there is one major difference between a cop and a coach and that is their approach in executing the five points listed:

a cop's approach is punitive, whereas a coach's approach is developmental. In other words, cops leverage their authority more to punish, and coaches apply theirs in order to help someone to grow. Coaches who fail to understand the difference between approaching people with a punitive versus a developmental mindset cross a line that makes it impossible to build and inspire a great team. They also tend to become abusers of people.

While you may have cop and coach tendencies that blend into your everyday leadership behaviors, there is normally one style that dominates. To help you evaluate yourself, consider these six signs that you're more cop than coach:

1. You spend more time looking for problems or mistakes your people make than seeking something positive to reinforce.
2. You have an enthusiasm for punishment. It feeds your ego and intoxicates you with power.
3. You use consequences more as a tool to humiliate rather than to improve performance.
4. You're more focused on keeping people in line than you are focused on helping them to grow.
5. You routinely rehearse people's past sins to them, dwelling in the past, rather than moving forward.
6. You care more about your rules than you do about relationships with your people.

As you read THE BOOK, you will find the "cop" approach used frequently by the Pharisees and made evident by their obsession with rituals, rules, and regulations. As they chastised and excommunicated the blind man healed at the Pool of Siloam, or brought the woman to Jesus who they "caught in the act" of adultery, you discern an unmistakable indifference toward people and apathy for their welfare. On the other hand, Jesus and the apostle Paul were stellar examples of coaches. They espoused clear behavioral guidelines and offered both positive reinforcement and confrontational feedback when necessary. They cared deeply for people as they served them, yet their primary concern was for their growth and not their comfort or happiness. Paradoxically, their followers were far happier and fulfilled, and they built teams that helped multiply their personal success and add value to all generations that followed them. Perhaps it's time to ditch your badge and club so that you may pick up your towel and basin.

SUMMARY

Hiring slow and strategically, defining reality in your organization, creating a high-accountability culture, and developing your inner circle are strategies you should give immediate attention to so that you can move your organization forward. However, they are not equally important. Here's why: If you don't have the right people to begin with, what good does it do to set expectations, try to hold them accountable, or spend time mentoring them? These efforts would be little more than an intellectual exercise without having hired right to begin with. After all, a great dream—your vision—with the wrong team is a nightmare! On the other hand, vision with the right strategy developed by and executed by incompetent people is a hallucination! Holding people accountable for objectives they are incapable of hitting is frustrating, exhausting, and cruel! And trying to build an inner circle from among the ranks of morons, misfits, or moochers is laughable! It all goes back to the right people, first! But to get the right people first, you must get right first! So we're right back to where we started in Chapter 1: learning leadership lessons from THE BOOK to improve yourself and elevate your own character and competence must precede trying to fix or improve the people around you. Keep this sequence in mind as you embark on your journey to greater organizational excellence and results. The trek to organizational growth will always start with you, and your enterprise will stop growing when you do.

REVELATION

The number one obstacle to developing an inner circle and elevating the discretion and abilities of your highest potential team members is your own ego. This is especially true if you are really good at what you do. Like many highly capable leaders, you may believe that as long as you're carrying the ball, everything will be all right. Thus, you'll hoard power, micromanage, and take for granted your top people. This would be an excellent time for an exercise in humility, where you search yourself for tendencies to build yourself up in order to keep others down. Most leaders would never intentionally abuse others in this manner, but they do so unconsciously to protect their own insecurities and need for recognition. In other words, the greatest obstacle to taking your team to the next level may not be their abilities at all. It may be your own selfishness and short-sightedness. If this is the case, face your flaws and fix them. For starters, re-read Chapter 3.

ACTION EXERCISE

FOUR STEPS TO BUILD YOUR TEAM BY THE BOOK

1. What can you do to begin hiring more slowly and strategically? Be specific and list at least two things.

   _____

2. Which aspect of reality is strongest/weakest in your organization? What can you do to improve each of the following areas?
   A. Vision:
   B. Core values:
   C. Performance expectations:

3. What is the first step you'll take to build a stronger accountability culture in your organization? Be specific.

   _____

4. Who makes up your inner circle? Who has the potential to become part of your inner circle? How can you take this person/people to a higher performance level?

   _____

CHAPTER 9

How to Lead Through Crisis

GENESIS

Like many Christians, I once had a sense of entitlement and believed that God owes us something as we go through tough times. After all, we tithe, pray, read His Word, and follow His commands, only to be blindsided by a crisis that pummels morale and paralyzes our organization. Doesn't our obedience protect us from downturns and setbacks? Not at all. In fact, the more I studied the Bible, the more clearly I saw that believers and heathen alike suffer during periods of crisis. Bills pile up, followers lose heart, and faith in a better tomorrow draws down. I learned that even highly placed and well developed leaders can feel alone and forgotten, or believe they're being punished for an old sin or unnecessarily tested during a crisis. Thus, the question is never when or if we will endure tough times in our personal lives and organizations. We absolutely will. The question is: How will we respond to the challenges? The way we respond to and endure through difficulties gives us the opportunity to demonstrate faith in God and apply His principles to our situation, rather than rack our brains trying to solve the situation on our own. There is no better biblical example of this than Job, and we can learn much from his life.

NINE LESSONS FROM THE LIFE OF JOB

Following are nine perspectives, lessons, and benefits from crises that can give us hope and strengthen our faith as we tackle the challenge of leading through crisis.

1. God doesn't owe an explanation to anyone when crisis hits. He is completely holy and will do what He deems right.

   Job observed:

   > In his hand is the life of every creature and the breath of all mankind. . . . To God belongs wisdom and power, counsel and understanding are his. What he tears down cannot be rebuilt; the man he imprisons cannot be released. If he holds back the waters, there is drought; if he lets them loose, they devastate the land. To him belong strength and victor; both deceived and deceiver are his. . . . He makes nations great, and destroys them; he enlarges nations and disperses them. (Job 12:10, 13–16, 23)

   Job knew enough about God to trust Him in the things he didn't know or understand. The more we know about God's history, character, and motives, the easier it is to accept what is happening to us, regardless of whether it makes sense in our own eyes.

2. God allows crises to increase our faith.[1]

   Ultimately, we need God far more than we need explanations from Him to our questions of "Why God?" Sometimes we need to get a larger view of God and of life. There are 155,000 people each day on earth that die. This fact should not astound us. What should amaze us is that more than six billion are allowed to continue living!

   For three dozen chapters, spanning months or even longer, God responded to Job's "why" questions with silence. When God eventually responded to Job He never answered his questions, but instead He gave a lesson in His almighty power. God's recitation of power increased Job's faith that God was in control, that He had a plan, and that He would sustain Job through his pain. It's important to remember that the presence of crises doesn't mark the absence of God.

3. God allows crises to humble us.[2]

Setbacks and suffering remind us of who we are and how vulnerable we remain. They also remind us of who we aren't, and what is beyond our control, and how limited our own power and possessions are in this grand universe. The ensuing humility and abandonment of independence and personal will are great benefits of affliction.

For this is what the high and lofty One says—He who lives forever, Whose name is holy, "I live in a high and holy place, but also with him who is contrite and lowly in spirit, to revive the spirit of the lowly and to revive the heart of the contrite" (Isaiah 57:15).

4. God allows crises in order to draw us nearer to Him.[3]

We experience God far more in tragedy than in triumph. Even after Job buried ten children at once, he cried out to God. He did not allow the pain of crisis to push him from God. Instead, he let it press him to God. God doesn't promise to keep us from crises, but He does promise to be with us during the tough times. Daniel's three friends weren't spared from the furnace any more than Daniel was from the lion's den. But God was with each during their trial, and saw them successfully through it.

5. God allows crises to make us more grateful.

Job said it best when chided by his wife and encouraged to curse God in the midst of their troubles: "We take the good days from God, why not also the bad days?" You may also recall that God eventually restored twice as much to Job as he lost. To put God's love and grace in perspective, we should never ask, "Why do bad things happen to good people?" Instead, we should stand in askance and awe and declare, "How do so many good things happen to us even when we're bad?"

6. God allows crises to prepare us for prosperity.[4]

   Without the growth and maturity that comes from pain, we are unprepared for prosperity. Perhaps there are no wiser words along these lines than these: Vast amounts of money, opportunities, and power ruin the unprepared.

7. God allows crises to demonstrate a greater revelation of Himself.

   God reveals Himself rather than reasons and explanations during a crisis. This helps us to advance from knowing merely about Him to truly knowing Him. *"My ears had heard of you, but now my eyes have seen you."* (Job 42:5)

8. God allows crises to teach us to pray and praise Him in anticipation of our deliverance and breakthrough. Praying and praising God before we see evidence of our breakthrough strengthens our faith in God and diminishes reliance on ourselves.[5]

   A. Jehosophat and his people praised God in the face of certain annihilation at the hands of Ammon, Moab, and Mount Seir, and soon saw victory!

      Now when they began to sing and to praise, the Lord
      set ambushes against the people of Ammon, Moab, and
      Mount Seir, who had come against Judah and they
      were defeated. (2 Chronicles 2:22)

   B. Facing an immense battle, Joshua and the Israelites shouted to God and blew the trumpets in anticipation of Jericho's walls coming down.

      So the people shouted when the priests blew the
      trumpets. And it happened when the people heard the
      sound of the trumpet, and the people shouted with a
      great shout, that the wall fell down flat. (Joshua 6:20)

   C. While in prison, Paul and Silas prayed and sang praises to God, after which their chains were loosed and the prison doors opened.

But at midnight, Paul and Silas were praying and singing hymns to God, and the prisoners were listening to them. Suddenly, there was a great earthquake, so that the foundations of the prison were shaken; and immediately all the doors were open and everyone's chains were unlocked. (Acts 16:25–26)

Note: The prayers and praises of Paul and Silas in the midst of their crisis didn't only benefit themselves. *All* those listening to them had their doors opened and chains loosed!

9. God allows crises to conform us more to Jesus' image.[6]

While most Christians are familiar with Romans 8:28, they often fail to connect it to the very next verse:

And we know that all things work together for good to those who love God, to those who are called according to His purpose." (Romans 8:28)

What is God's purpose?

For whom He foreknew, He also predestined to be conformed to the image of His Son . . ." (Romans 8:29)

God's desire is to shape our character to parallel His Son's. Through hardships, God chisels away from our lives all characteristics that keep us from being like Christ. This includes things like self-centeredness, pride, envy, selfishness, indifference, self-sufficiency, self-righteousness, greed, lust, and arrogance. It is only as we become more like Christ that we can do more for Christ and His people. Thus, God allows suffering to equip us for bigger and greater things! In order to make a difference as a leader, the *becoming* more must precede doing more. You can't export to others what you don't have. Nor can you take them on a journey you've never been on.

By THE BOOK Blessing

Throughout the Scriptures, miracle after miracle followed on the heels of a crisis! The biblical record is quite clear. There are no miracles without previous messes. The need for a miracle is necessitated by the presence of an impossible situation, usually unbearable sufferings.

—David Earley, *21 Reasons Bad Things Happen to Good People*
(Barbour Publishing, 2007)

Examples of the "Mess Before the Miracle"[7]

- Moses was leading the Israelites to their slaughter at the hands of Pharaoh *before* the Red Sea opened, allowing them to pass through.
- The multitude had to grow hungry and weary on two occasions *before* Jesus multiplied the fish and bread to feed them!
- Daniel was thrown into the lion's den *before* he could be spared and bring glory to God before the king.
- Shadrach, Meshach, and Abednego had to be placed inside the burning furnace *before* they could emerge without as much as a scent of smoke upon their beings.
- The widow and her son had to be starving *before* the unlimited flour and jar of oil were provided. Yet the staples both ran out when no longer needed.
- Peter had to go to prison *before* the angel could set him free.
- Lazarus had to die *before* he was raised from the dead.
- Jarius' daughter had to die *before* she was raised from the dead.
- The disciples had to completely fail on an all-night fishing expedition *before* Jesus filled their nets with an enormous catch.
- The storm had to scare the disciples into a panic *before* Jesus calmed the wind and waves.

- The woman had to bleed for 12 years *before* Jesus healed her with a simple touch.
- The 10 lepers had to experience the pain and humiliation of leprosy *before* they could experience the miracle of their healing.
- Bartimaeus had to endure a lifetime of blindness *before* experiencing a healing touch from the Great Physician.
- Jesus had to suffer the horrors of crucifixion *before* He was raised from the dead.

As God continues to conform you to Christ's image, pray that through His grace you may begin to face crises with a new strength and hope; considering them less a price you are paying and more of a prelude to the miraculous.

By THE BOOK Blessing

My ears had heard of you, but now my eyes have seen you. (Job 42:5)

FIVE CAUSES AND CONSEQUENCES OF CRISES

When crisis strikes, you cannot expect to reverse your fortunes with a *business as usual* approach. In other words, you cannot go from break-even to breakthrough without *breaking from* the contrary conditions that have rendered you as reactionary, panicked, or static. There are two primary categories of actions that can create crises for leaders: externally induced and internally bred. In this section, I primarily address leading through crisis when the crisis is not of your own making but thrust upon you by conditions beyond your control. Following is a series of proactive steps you can take to lead effectively through challenging times and reestablish the momentum, morale, and results necessary to grow your organization.

COMMON EXTERNAL CAUSES THAT CREATE INTERNAL CRISIS WITHIN ORGANIZATIONS

- Political unrest.
- Economic upheaval.
- Natural disasters.
- Aggressive competition.
- Sudden or unexpected loss of an organization's leadership.

Since there is little you can do to affect these factors, it is best to limit the time you dwell on or are distracted by them. However, since it is helpful to be aware of some potential consequences of externally induced crises, I present some in the next section.

Five Common Consequences of Externally Induced Crises

1. Loss of or unclear mission and/or vision.

   This concerns what your organization stands for and where it is going, in the most precise terms possible. Without a common purpose and direction that creates unity and passion, different leaders—pursuing separate agendas—create constant chaos.

2. Loss of focus.

   In an attempt to regroup, it is common to lose focus and drift from your strengths, spread limited resources too thin, and marginalize your personal and corporate talents as you endeavor to find your way.

3. Loss of momentum.

   Once you lose your momentum, the impact of every subsequent setback is exaggerated. You lose your optimism and develop an expectancy that something else bad is about to happen. In attempting to regain your momentum you are prone to overreach with long-shot, low-probability-of-success heroics.

4. Loss of courage.

   Loss of courage involves three things: fear of risk, resistance to change, and reluctance to spend. You're no longer stretching, you're

214

maintaining. You play not to lose, rather than play to win. You become so obsessed with not giving additional ground that the ground you're standing on becomes quicksand, rendering you largely irrelevant.

5. Diminished morale.

There is little energy or joy within the organization. In fact, there is chaos in the cubicles as constituents feel hopeless, lost, overwhelmed, and sink into survival mode. People are prone to believe that their best days are behind them.

The silver lining: The good news is that with robust leadership you can positively affect each of these five situations, and doing so will serve as a catalyst to jump-starting a breakthrough of renewed growth and vitality within your organization.

LEADERSHIP STEPS TO ADDRESS THE FIVE COMMON CONSEQUENCES OF CRISIS

1. LOSS OF OR UNCLEAR MISSION AND/OR VISION

Redefine your purpose and direction: a.k.a. mission and vision. This means you create and communicate precise, concise, one- to two-sentence descriptions of both your purpose and your direction (your mission and your vision). Your vision should contain bold and measurable components to be accomplished within a predetermined time frame. The specific nature of the vision creates the means to convert a cause into a campaign. It fosters accountability and offers the team clear objectives to rally around. This creates unity and purpose that quickly awaken a sleepy culture.

Especially in a crisis, it is wise to underpin your new vision with a series of short-term goals. Short-term goals create a positive pressure to shake off lethargy, liberate you from crises-induced immobility, refocus on the future, and make something happen NOW! Especially in times of crisis, there is power in NOW! A long-term vision without short-term objectives takes the pressure off of doing anything today!

While there are many things you can delegate as a leader, defining mission and vision are not among them. It is the leader's privilege and responsibility to define what the future will look like, to align people with that picture, and to inspire them to make it happen despite the crisis. Get clear about what you want and where you're going! If there is a mist in the pulpit, there'll be a fog in the pews.

Once you cast or redefine your vision, it's easier to stay focused on what matters most. When you're clear about what you want, it's easier to know what to say "yes" to, "no" to, what to include, and what to discard. Laser-like focus is essential during a crisis.

By THE BOOK Blessing

I'm doing a great work and I can't come down. (Nehemiah 6:3)

---

2. LOSS OF FOCUS

In order to lead well through times of crises, you must build your efforts upon a foundation of strengths. This includes returning your focus, time, and energies to personal, team, and corporate core competencies. Recommit to your personal core competencies and invest your time, energy, and resources into these areas.

In times of crisis, leaders tend to spend more time plugging holes and doing damage control than they do leading. They invest more hours charting results than charting the course. Spending time majoring in minor things may get you by, but working within the parameters of your personal strengths will get you great. Get back in your core competence zone and stay there!

In addition to your personal strengths, you must identify your organizational core competencies and rebuild upon those pillars of strength. Crises can cause you to chase silver bullets and quick fixes. This departure from sound basics and disciplines can convert your rut into a grave. Refocus on what you do best. You cannot restart momentum by wallowing in areas where you are marginal.

As you refocus on personal and corporate strengths, it is also essential that you reinvigorate your core people, as they are the key to getting you through a crisis. You successfully emerge from a crisis on the backs of your best performing, most talented people, not on the shoulders of your weakest links. Give more time, attention, and support to the people you count on most. Don't take your top people for granted during a crisis as you try and motivate the bottom dwellers, most of whom inflict a negative value upon your organization during challenging times.

3. LOSS OF MOMENTUM

It is a common, but grave, leadership mistake to wait for a change in outside conditions to create internal momentum for your organization. This is unwise, because waiting for something to happen from the outside-in reduces you to "victim" status because what you're hoping for is outside of your control. Besides, if you rely on external factors to create momentum, as soon as they dissipate, so does your momentum! To lead effectively through crisis you must create organizational momentum from the inside out. One of the best strategies for accomplishing this is to install more structure within your culture. Structure creates internal energy that generates momentum. Structure can include everything from daily goals, to early morning "war room" strategy meetings, "X" number of contacts/ phone calls/mailers per day, daily training sessions, scheduled one-on-one coaching sessions with team members, and the like.

Frankly, structure puts people into motion and keeps them there. Without intensified internal structure, people spend too much time waiting, wondering, and worrying. Structure helps turn their downtime into prime time. Without purposeful daily structure, people can begin to treat a crisis like it's business as usual rather than a temporary anomaly that will soon be overcome.

Strategies for Restarting Momentum

- Regroup and refocus your team by selecting or redefining a vision, and assembling a plan to attack it. You must clearly state your objective. Even the most able team members can't focus their minds and clearly state an objective in crisis without a very deliberate intent.

217

Regaining your sense of purpose and vision serves as a catalyst for momentum.

- Quickly, loudly, and publicly—positively reinforce the behaviors and results you're looking for and that will help you reach your objectives.

Reinforced people reinforce other people. The chain reaction transforms a sleepy culture and reignites momentum.

- Set up short-term wins and celebrate each victory along the way.

Nothing silences cynics like results! Short-term wins help bring the stragglers along. You can produce short-term wins by setting daily goals and then pulling out all the stops to achieve them.

- Redouble your efforts to focus people on what they can control.

A victim's mindset drains momentum and morale. Don't permit it! Even in the toughest of times people can control their attitude, character choices, work ethic, level of discipline, where they spend their time, and with whom they spend their time. The more everyone focuses on the aspects of their job that they can control, the less things they cannot control will affect them.

- Individually sit down with each team member and redefine performance expectations.

Performance expectations can become cloudy or conveniently forgotten during times of crisis. By showing each team member what is expected of them as an individual, you make it personal and create a benchmark for accountability.

- If conditions make it improbable that you will see meaningful results any time soon, focus people on activity goals that will eventually lead to the results.

Keeping people focused on the right activities maintains discipline and morale—people feel better about themselves and their situation when they are doing something about it.

- Develop yourself in the down times.

Work harder on yourself in areas of personal growth and spiritual disciplines during a crisis. This helps maintain your own passion and momentum, which positively rubs off on the team.

- Don't let up on accountability during tough times. Even if it's more difficult to hold people accountable for tangible results, you should hold them accountable for executing prescribed activities. Failing to do so will weaken your culture and make it less likely that you will rebound.

  Crises cannot be interpreted by team members as a permission slip to stop working hard and being productive.

By THE BOOK Blessing

We are hard pressed on every side, yet not crushed; we are perplexed but not in despair; persecuted but not forsaken, struck down but not destroyed . . . (2 Corinthians 4:8–9)

---

4. LOSS OF COURAGE

When the bottom falls out, it's easy to lose your killer instinct as an organization and climb into the bunker to wait for the shelling to stop. However, passivity prolongs the duration of a crisis, whereas proactivity will shorten the duration of a crisis. In times of crisis, you can't wait your way out or wish your way out, you must work your way out!

Loss of courage during a crisis often manifests in the following three ways:

- Fear of risk.

  It is often necessary to take mature risks to regain ground during or after a crisis. Too often, a crisis can cause leaders to commit the sin of living defensively. A mature risk is one that is executed in an area of strength. It seizes an opportunity when there is more to gain than to lose by trying. A mature risk is not without the possibility of loss. However, the leader knows that it is time to move forward once the cost of comfortable inaction outweighs the cost of trying and falling short. Just pursuing a mature risk helps you regain the upper hand in your organization, restart momentum, and elevate

morale because people are energized by the fact they are doing
something to reverse their fortunes.

- Resistance to change.

    Leaders can regain traction and awaken a subdued culture by
changing the things around them rather than by waiting for the
things around them to change. The change may involve personnel,
redefined expectations or vision, the elimination of red tape, the
suspension of cumbersome rules, the empowerment of front-line
employees, and other actions that improve an organization's ability
to move quickly and effectively in the midst of a crisis.

- Reluctance to spend.

    The most common areas where leaders become reluctant to
spend during a crisis are training and marketing. However, you
cannot cut your capacity to produce and expect to sustain or
increase production. Even if funds are not available in areas like
training and marketing, you should commit to spending more time
in these areas. After all, a crisis often reduces the number of
opportunities an organization has to increase sales or market share.
Thus, employees must become more highly skilled so that they are
able to maximize the fewer opportunities they're seeing.

5. Diminished Morale

As you follow the remedies to address loss of vision, loss of focus, loss of
momentum, and loss of nerve, morale will elevate quickly and measurably
as a natural consequence of your bold and inspiring leadership.

Fifteen Steps to Stay Up in Down Times

In addition to addressing the five common consequences of crises, there
are fifteen other effective actions leaders should take to lead well during
crises:

1. LEAD FROM THE FRONT AND BECOME MORE DECISIVE

In periods of crises, when followers don't see or hear from the leader, they tend to lose hope. You must remain visible, accessible, inspirational, and instructional. Eventually, this makes you unstoppable! On the other hand, when you are invisible during a crisis your leadership credibility is reduced to the ridiculous.

> It is impossible to be aloof and remain effective at the same time.
>
> —*General George Patton*

In times of crises, leaders show up! Effective crises leaders understand that they cannot rebuild momentum and morale in their organization by memo, voice mail, e-mail, or text message. They must show up and lead!

The biggest problem with leaders in a time of crisis is that they don't lead! They tweak, tinker, tamper, manage, massage, maintain, administer, and preside. But they impact no one and add value to nothing! They talk like leaders but act like anchors. At best they are ceremonial leaders, mere pretenders with titles who inflict irreversible damage upon their people and organization. It is only when leading from the front that leaders can make the fast decisions necessary to reverse losses or seize opportunities.

> In tougher times, leaders must be able to turn on a dime. They must become more decisive. When the ship is going down, the captain doesn't call a meeting, he gives an order.
>
> —*Peter Drucker*

2. REDEFINE PERFORMANCE AND BEHAVIORAL EXPECTATIONS

Along with mission and vision, performance and behavioral expectations must be redefined. People must know what is expected of them and by when, as well as the consequences for failing to deliver. Vision serves as a "velvet glove," whereas performance and behavioral expectations exhibit more of an "iron fist." A combination of both is necessary to inspire the action and effort necessary to change the status quo.

You must be "part Zechariah, part Haggai" to redirect people's focus to what is expected and then shake them out of their funk by giving them a swift kick in the backside to get them moving in the right direction.

> As leader, you can afford to be wrong, but you cannot
> afford to be unclear.
>
> —*Andy Stanley*

3. Clear Out the Dead Weight

Face reality concerning each team member by applying zero-based thinking. This strategy means that you ask the following question concerning each team member: "Knowing what I now know about this person, if they applied for the job today, would I rehire him or her?" If the answer is "no," then you have an unacceptable situation that must be dealt with. Because there is less margin for error in times of crisis, you do not have the luxury of coddling underperformers. By keeping nonperformers on your team, you commit the leadership sin of weakening the strong in order to strengthen the weak.

4. Cut Once and Cut All

If you cut expenses, get it over with! Dragging out expense reduction is like water torture that continues to distract, demoralize, and deplete your people. It's also important to bring closure after cuts. Explain to everyone what was done, why it was done, and how the organization is healthier and jobs are safer as a result. Then refocus again on what's ahead of you.

5. Remember and Apply the 80/20 Rule

Eighty percent of what holds you back from moving forward and regaining momentum is within your control and 20 percent is not. The 80 percent is rooted in inside decisions. The 20 percent is comprised of outside conditions. The more you focus on making better decisions, the less relevant the conditions beyond your control become. During a crisis, severe conditions often plunge you into dire straits. But it'll be the quality and consistency of right decisions that creates your rebound.

6. Learn from the Past

A downturn will always expose the sins of the good times. Use crises to acknowledge cracks in your organization's foundation, and resolve to correct them so that you emerge from a crisis stronger and less vulnerable to a future disaster than you were before the crisis struck. Bonding with or rehearsing mistakes will exacerbate the effects of the crisis, as they drain and demoralize you. Let go and move on!

7. Encourage Conflict Before Making Big Decisions

While making faster decisions during a crisis is essential, they must not be reckless. Thus, you must encourage conflict and dissent from your leadership team to determine the best course, because conflict brings forth clarity. Conflict ensures every side of an issue is examined. It destroys groupthink and uncovers blind spots. Too much harmony is cancerous to decision making! And the bigger the decision, risk, or opportunity, the more conflict you need! This is not an excuse to delay, but an invitation to debate and then decide.

8. Tighten Financial Controls

If there is one sector where it is appropriate to micromanage during a crisis, it is in the area of finances. Precious resources must be fully leveraged and maximized throughout your recovery and beyond. One of your key responsibilities during a crisis is to preserve cash. Keep in mind that organizations can be profitable and still go bankrupt; earnings don't keep you in business, cash does!

9. Empower Your People

If there is one sector where it is appropriate to loosen up and give added discretion in a crisis, it is in the area of associate empowerment. Follow the wisdom of Matthew 25, and the Parable of the Talents, and increase latitude, push down power, and allocate opportunities in accordance with people's abilities and not equally across the board. This strategy should be applied only after the vision, mission, and performance expectations have been clearly redefined. Empowerment without clarity creates chaos.

10. Invest in and Depend More on Your Team, Especially Your Inner Circle

The natural tendency in a crisis is to look inward rather than outward for help. Leaders begin to depend too much on themselves and can become overwhelmed and ineffective. The opposite must happen. Accelerate the development of your team and rely more on them. Challenge them to step up and demonstrate greater leadership.

The paradox of power states that in order to become more powerful, you must give power away. Hoarding power actually makes you less powerful because you become overwhelmed and ineffective. Giving it away multiples your power as a leader because you empower those closest to you to operate at higher performance levels. In a crisis, decentralizing power is essential to becoming more nimble and responsive to conditions as they develop.

11. DEMONSTRATE EMOTIONAL CONTROL

The speed of the leader is the speed of the pack. Your attitude, reactions, body language, and disposition will demonstrate more to your followers than mere words. As a leader in crisis, you are on display. Everything you say has the potential to elevate or devastate, to earn respect or lose it, to enhance your presence or cheapen it. A key to emotional control is to make the habit of increasing the space between a provocation and your response to it!

By THE BOOK Blessing

He who answers a matter before he hears it, it is folly and shame for him. (Proverbs 18:13)

He who controls his anger is better than the mighty, and he who rules his spirit, than he who takes a city. (Proverbs 16:32)

There is little that provides a greater distraction and momentum-breaker than a leader who cannot publicly control his emotions and attitude. During times of crisis, this character flaw has a devastating effect on morale. Especially during a crisis, you must lead deliberately and not do what comes naturally.

12. EARN THE RIGHT TO BECOME OPTIMISTIC ABOUT THE FUTURE!

Legitimate optimism is built upon a foundation of preparation. Without preparation, you're not an optimist, you're a daydreamer. While a clear goal for your organization is essential, vision without strategy is hallucination. Remember, David had a vision to defeat Goliath, but he also had a plan. He stopped by the stream to pick up five stones for the battle. As you face your Goliath, do you have your "five stones"?

13. Communicate Honestly, Openly, and Often

When followers don't hear from the leader during a crisis they assume the worst. "No news" is not good news. Leaders instill confidence in followers when they make an earnest effort to let them in on things during tough times. Acknowledge the severity of the crisis, demonstrate unshakeable confidence that you will prevail, and communicate your plan of action. For an example on how to do this, read Acts 27:13–26, in which the Apostle Paul addresses the crew during the tempest.

14. Involve Others in Devising the Strategy for Rebounding and Reaching Your Vision

It is not necessary or desirable for the leaders to devise the organization's recovery strategy on their own. Rather, the leader's job is to create the context for others to contribute to the content of the strategy. People support what they help create, but they've got to weigh-in before they buy-in.

15. Seize the Opportunity to Make a Difference!

Crises offer a unique opportunity for leaders to demonstrate their mettle. They have the chance to uplift, to rebuild, to inspire, to empower, to teach, and to make a significant difference in the lives of their followers. If you are in a leadership position when a crisis strikes, you should pray that God has you there for a reason, just as He did with Joseph and Esther. Trust His wisdom and plans more than your instincts and experience.

By THE BOOK Blessing

. . . yet who knows whether you have come to the kingdom for such a time as this. (Esther 4:14)

By THE BOOK Lesson in Leadership

Nehemiah Leads Through Crisis

The story of Nehemiah spearheading the rebuilding of the Jerusalem Wall is a textbook manual in leading through crisis. Learn from his strategy and actions. Here's his blueprint that you can use today:

1. Earn the buy-in of followers for why action is important.

Then, discuss what you will do to remedy the situation. Keep it simple, make your objective clear and concise so that it is easy for people to understand and rally around. People cannot be aggressive when they are confused.

> Come let us build the wall of Jerusalem, that we may no longer be a reproach. (Nehemiah 2:17)

Make certain that reasons precede mandates. People can live with the "what and how" if they understand the "why." The "why" gives them pull power through the difficult times. Here are the reasons Nehemiah presented to those he wished to enlist in his cause:

- Nehemiah had committed himself to oversee the project (2:5).
- Asaph had approved timber and lumber for the gate (2:8).
- The situation was a reproach to Israel (2:17).
- The ruined walls could not protect any of them (2:17).
- God's hand was on him and had given him favor (2:18).
- King Artaxerxes had given him permission to come and rebuild (2:18).

2. Remain visible and accessible.

This is a recurring theme in this chapter, and it's no coincidence. This is an essential discipline. Throughout the rebuilding, Nehemiah was in the trenches with his people. In times of crisis, effective leaders show up! They do not hide!

3. Keep others busy with productive tasks that allow them to take ownership of the vision.

> After him Benjamin and Hasshub made repairs opposite their house. After them Azariah the son of Maasiah, the son of Ananiah, made repairs by their house. (Nehemiah 3:23)

Remember: A sense of ownership determines whether followers comply with, or commit to, a cause.

4. Focus like a laser-beam on the task at hand and on the desired results.

> . . . that Sanballat and Geshem sent to me, saying, "Come, let us meet together among the villages in the plain of Ono." But they thought to do me harm. So I sent messengers to them, saying, "I am doing a great work, so that I cannot come down. Why should the work cease while I leave it and go down to you?" But they sent me this message four times, and I answered them in the same manner." (Nehemiah 6:2–4)

When you are rebuilding after a crisis, there is much you will have to give up in order to go up: certain tasks, people, habits, and mindsets.

5. Survive success.

The Jerusalem Wall was rebuilt in 52 days . . . after being broken down for 123 years! This remarkable accomplishment was followed by a letdown. The same thing happens in organizations today when leaders don't renew, enlarge, or build a new vision upon prior accomplishments. When this occurs, a calm contentment, a smug satisfaction, sets in that creates a sense of complacency. Organizations fail to maintain momentum after a rebound because of their chronic inconsistency. Be aware of this pitfall and overcome it.

SHINE THE LIGHT

As a business consultant to numerous companies during an array of crises, I've noticed the following common leadership flaws exhibited by leaders at all levels during crises. I've included action lessons to help you overcome these shortcomings:

1. The leaders develop a "bunker mentality," which causes temporary paralysis. They become immobile and go into a "wait" mode. They wait for the things around them to change rather than changing the things around them.

   Action lesson: You can't wait your way out of a crisis or wish your way out of a crisis. You must work your way out of a crisis!

2. The leaders stop leading. During a crisis, many leaders become less visible and accessible, poring over data and reports and reacting, rather than leading from the front and staying in the trenches with their team.

   Action lesson: Passivity will prolong the duration of a crisis, whereas proactivity shortens the duration of a crisis. You must remain more visible, accessible, instructional, and inspirational. When your people don't hear from you or see you during tough times, they assume the worst.

3. The leaders stop holding others accountable, weakening their culture and exacerbating damage to morale and momentum.

   Action lesson: Set shorter-term activity and results goals and hold others accountable for hitting them. This creates energy and momentum, even during slow or confused times. It also maintains discipline and heightens morale as people feel better about themselves when they are doing *something* to change their fortunes.

4. The leaders fail to honor commitments they made prior to the crisis. This dishonors and displeases God. It demonstrates a faith void in God's ability to take care of you if you behave honorably and is clear evidence that you've abandoned God and have chosen to rely on your own wisdom.

   Action lesson: Do what is right without excuse and regardless of the cost. This honors God and helps you to remain bless-able.

To sum it up, the most important thing for you to do during a crisis is to be led by God as you continue to lead.

SUMMARY

While the steps offered in this chapter are essential to helping you to lead successfully through the crises you will encounter throughout your career, they are not intended to create a sense of self-assurance that may cause you to depend too much upon yourself and your own abilities. You must, of course, fulfill your leadership responsibilities with excellence, integrity, and resolve. But your most important duties during a crisis are to seek God's wisdom, petition His mercy and grace, and trust His faithfulness.

REVELATION

This chapter has offered many proactive steps for you to take during a crisis. One size does not fit all. There is no standard, step-by-step manual that can help you navigate successfully through all crises. To use a football term, you must call the plays based on where you're at on the field. In other words, adapt your style and strategy to fit the crisis rather than trying to squeeze the crisis through your canned, panned approach. Stay focused on a successful outcome while remaining flexible in your approach. In other words, don't fall in love with your plan! While commitment is noble, rigidity is not.

CLOSING THOUGHTS

I have no way of knowing what you have gotten from this book or how it will benefit you. Time will tell. My hope is that these words fell on good ground and will not be taken away by the birds of this world that would devour them, or rendered ineffective and shallow by a stony heart, or that they do not create an instant surge of enthusiasm that soon becomes choked out by the "get it done at any cost" mindset of the world. Jesus' parable about these scenarios bears repeating as our time together draws to a close:

Then He spoke many things to them in parables, saying, "Behold, a sower went out to sow. And as he sowed, some seed fell by the wayside; and the birds came and devoured them. Some fell on the stony places, where they did not have much earth; and they immediately sprang up because they had no depth of earth. But when the sun was up they were scorched, and because they had no root they withered away. And some fell among thorns, and the thorns sprang up and choked them. But others fell on good ground and yielded a crop: some a hundred fold some sixty, some thirty. He who has ears to hear, let him hear!" (Matthew 13:3–9)

My hope for you is that you are a hundred-fold reader! That you will not wait for the things around you to change, but that you will instead begin to change the things around you! To help you and your team with your personal development journey, I will give you a free annual subscription to our *How to Run Your Business by THE BOOK* monthly newsletter! Just write me at dave@learntolead.com and include the words "By THE BOOK NL" in the subject line. Each month's issue comes digitally so that you can e-mail it to your friends and associates. We also include an audio file of the newsletter that you can download onto your computer or your MP3 player. I'll leave you with three final scriptures to help you to stay on course as you run your business by THE BOOK:

1. *"Be imitators of God. For you were once darkness, but now you are light in the Lord. Walk as children of the light."* (Ephesians 5:1, 8)
2. *"Let this mind be in you which was also in Christ Jesus . . ."* (Philippians 2:5)
3. *"Therefore we must give more earnest heed to the things we have heard, lest we drift away."* (Hebrews 2:1)

ACTION EXERCISE

THREE STEPS TO LEAD THROUGH CRISIS

1. What have you learned in this book that can help you prevent an internally induced crisis in your organization? What will you do with this information?

   _____

2. Which 3 of the 15 steps offered do you believe will most help you through the crises you face in your organization?
3. What do you see as your number one leadership responsibility during a crisis?

   _____

Quick Scriptural Reference Guide by THE BOOK

1. Can you teach talent? James 1:17
2. If you're younger than someone you supervise, how do you confront them? I Timothy 5:1
3. What is the best advice you could give a young leader? I Timothy 4:12
4. How important is it to stop gossip fast? II Timothy 2:16; Proverbs 26:20
5. How important is it to associate with the right peers at work? Proverbs 12:20, 13:26; I Corinthians 15:33
6. What is at the core of most organizational strife? Proverbs 13:10
7. What is the key to success in my position? Proverbs 22:4
8. Should I partner with someone who doesn't share my own values? II Chronicles 20:37
9. How can leaders attract better followers? Matthew 7:17

10. Is it true that leaders are to be held to a higher standard than followers? James 3:1
11. What is the maximum number of times I should allow someone to violate my values before removing them? Titus 3:10; Proverbs 22:10
12. What should be the consequence for someone on the team who doesn't do his or her share? II Thessalonians 3:10
13. What are some tips for communicating effectively with people? Proverbs 18:13, 29:20; James 1:17; Matthew 12:36–37
14. How should I accept feedback on my performance? Proverbs 12:1, 13:18; Hebrews 11:13
15. How should I answer questions from a fool? Proverbs 26:4, 23:9
16. What is the best way to defuse a harsh accusation against me? Proverbs 15:1
17. How should I feel about competitors/peers who get ahead in business dishonestly? Proverbs 13:11, 24:19–20; Isaiah 5:20
18. Should I wait for the "perfect" time to act or make a decision? Ecclesiastes 11:4
19. Should I distribute pay, bonuses, and other perks equally across all team members in the interest of fairness? Matthew 25:12–28
20. How important is positive reinforcement, and how fast should I give it? Proverbs 3:27; Hebrews 12:11
21. How important is it to "choose my battles"? 2 Timothy 2:23
22. Should making money be my primary motivator in business? Ecclesiastes 5:10
23. Should I be reserved in my leadership style or wear my emotions on my sleeve? Proverbs 14:29, 16:32, 19:11, 25:28
24. How should I respond when my competitor fails? Proverbs 24:17–18
25. Are there any jobs in a workplace that are too lowly? Proverbs 14:23
26. Is it okay to spend more time with my highest potential people, or should I spend most of my time with strugglers? Matthew 17:28; Mark 14:33; Luke 8:51
27. If my workplace's values contradict what I believe biblically, what should I do? I Corinthians 2:5; Acts 4:19; Ephesians 5:11

28. What is the best way to get to the top of my organization? Mark 9:35, 10:43–44
29. Is it acceptable to get publicly angry on the job in order to make a point? Ephesians 4:26–27
30. Is it possible that my boss/peers won't accept me or understand me because they are not Christians or don't believe in the Bible? I Corinthians 2:14
31. How do I respond to someone who does me wrong in the workplace? Romans 12:17, 12:19–21; I Thessalonians 5:15
32. If I used to hang around with the "rough" crowd and now I disassociate myself with them, what might happen, good or bad? Isaiah 59:15; I Peter 4:4; Mark 4:21–22
33. What is a good daily discipline to prepare for the day and/or to do throughout the course of the day? Mark 1:35; I Thessalonians 5:14–22
34. In today's business world, isn't it okay to self-promote myself in order to get noticed by the higher-ups? Proverbs 25:6–7, 27:2; Matthew 23:12
35. Isn't it natural to have anxiety about how business is going and to be apprehensive about hitting our numbers? Luke 12:29–31; Philippians 4:6–7; Isaiah 26:3
36. I really don't like my boss/the job I'm working on/my company, and so on. How am I supposed to handle this? Colossians 3:23–24
37. How do I handle the people in the workplace who are out to hurt my career or damage my reputation? Proverbs 3:25–26, 21:7
38. I don't feel qualified to make some of the decisions I face. What do I do? James 1:5–6
39. Should I rely on others or become more dependent upon myself? Ecclesiastes 4:9–12
40. How can I expect people to respond to training? Matthew 13:3–9
41. If I know what I should do but don't do it, is it as wrong as doing something bad deliberately? James 4:17; Matthew 25:45
42. Is it true that in business I should never be satisfied? Hebrews 13:5

Notes

Chapter 1

1. Charles Swindoll, *Paul* (Nashville, TN: Thomas Nelson Publishers, 2002), pp. 46–47.
2. Ibid., p. 82.
3. Ibid., p. 43.

Chapter 3

1. www.brainyquote.com/quotes/authors/h/henry_ward_beecher.html.
2. Wayne Mack with Joshua Mack, *Humility: The Forgotten Virtue* (Phillipsburg, NJ: P&R Publishing, 2005).
3. Ibid.
4. www.spurgeon.org/sermons/0097.htm.
5. Wayne Mack with Joshua Mack, *Humility: The Forgotten Virtue* (Phillipsburg, NJ: P&R Publishing, 2005).
6. Ibid.
7. Ibid.
8. Ibid.
9. Ibid.

10. Ibid.
11. Ibid.
12. Ibid.
13. Ibid.
14. www.brainyquote.com/quotes/authors/c/charles_spurgeon.html.
15. Wayne Mack with Joshua Mack, *Humility: The Forgotten Virtue* (Phillipsburg, NJ: P&R Publishing, 2005).
16. Ibid.
17. Ibid.
18. Ibid.
19. http://dailychristianquote.com/dcqpride.html.
20. Wayne Mack with Joshua Mack, *Humility: The Forgotten Virtue* (Phillipsburg, NJ: P&R Publishing, 2005).
21. Ibid.
22. C. J. Mahaney, *Humility: True Greatness* (Colorado Springs, CO: Multnomah, 2005), p. 21.

Chapter 5

1. C. Bernard Ruffin, *The Twelve* (Huntington, IN: Our Sunday Visitor Publishing Division, 1997), pp. 67–70.
2. Ibid.
3. Ibid.
4. Ibid.
5. Ibid.
6. Ibid.
7. Ibid.

Chapter 7

1. Bill Gothard and Jim Sammons, *The Men's Manual Volume II* (Oakbrook, IL: Institute of Basic Life Principles Inc., 1983), pp. 78.
2. Ibid.
3. Ibid.
4. Ibid.
5. Ibid.
6. Ibid.

7. Ibid.
8. Ibid.
9. Ibid.
10. Ibid.
11. Ibid.
12. Ibid.
13. Ibid.
14. Ibid.
15. Ibid.
16. Ibid.
17. Tom Carter, *Spurgeon's Commentary on Great Chapters of the Bible* (Grand Rapids, MI: Kregel Publications, 1998), p. 31.
18. Ibid., p. 32.
19. Ibid., p. 31.

Chapter 9

1. Dave Earley, *21 Reasons Bad Things Happen to Good People* (Uhrichsville, OH: Barbour Publishing, 2007), p. 30.
2. Ibid., p. 37.
3. Ibid., p. 43.
4. Ibid., p. 50.
5. Ibid., p. 64.
6. Ibid., p. 100.
7. Ibid., pp. 65–66.

References

Carter, Tom. 1998. *Spurgeon's Commentary on Great Chapters of the Bible.* Grand Rapids, MI: Kregel Publications.

Daily Success Scripture Meditation. 1985. Oak Brook, IL: Institute of Basic Life Principles.

Earley, Dave. 2007. *21 Reasons Bad Things Happen to Good People.* Uhrichsville, OH: Barbour Publishing.

Fontenot, Michael, and Thomas Jones. 2003. *The Prideful Soul's Guide to Humility.* Billerica, MA: Discipleship Publications International.

Foxe, John. 2007. *Foxe's Voices of the Martyrs.* Orlando, FL: Bridge-Logos Publishing.

Gothard, Bill, and Jim Sammons. 1983. *Men's Manual Volume II.* Oak Brook, IL: Institute of Basic Life Principles.

Mack, Wayne, and Joshua Mack. 2005. *Humility: The Forgotten Virtue.* Phillipsburg, NJ: P&R Publishing.

Mahaney, C. J. 2005. *Humility: True Greatness.* Colorado Springs, CO: Multnomah Books.

Maxwell, John, Executive Editor. 2002. *The Maxwell Leadership Bible New King James Version.* Nashville, TN: Thomas Nelson Publishers.

Murray, Andrew. 2001. *Humility: The Journey Toward Holiness*. Bloomington, MN: Bethany House Publishers.

Nightingale, Earl. 1978. *Earl Nightingale on Winning: The Common Denominator of Success* (audiobook). Niles, IL: Nightingale-Conant Corp.

Prince, Derek. 2002. *God's Will for Your Life*. New Kensington, PA: Whitaker House.

Richards, Larry. 2002. *365 Day Daily Devotional Commentary for Living Christian Software*. Libronix.

Ruffin, Bernard. 1997. *The Twelve: Lives of the Apostles after Calvary*. Huntington, IN: Our Sunday Visitor Publishing.

Stanley, Andy, and Reggie Joiner. 2004. *Discovering God's Will*. Colorado Springs, CO: Multnomah Books.

Swindoll, Charles. 2002. *Paul*. Nashville, TN: Thomas Nelson Publishers.

About the Author

Dave Anderson is president of LearnToLead, a sales and leadership training company based near Los Angeles, California. He has given leadership presentations in 14 countries and speaks more than 100 times per year. Dave has written numerous books. His other Wiley titles include *Up Your Business*, *If You Don't Make Waves You'll Drown*, *How to Deal with Difficult Customers*, *The TKO Business* series, *How to Lead by THE BOOK*. His articles and interviews have appeared in hundreds of publications worldwide, including the *Wall Street Journal* and *Investor's Daily*. Dave authors a monthly leadership column for two nationwide magazines and is a frequent panelist on MSNBC's *Your Business*. With his wife, Rhonda, Dave is cofounder of The Matthew 25:35 Foundation, a nonprofit organization that helps to educate, feed, heal, and house indigent people throughout the world.

To view and use hundreds of free video clips and personal development and training articles, visit www.learntolead.com. To book Dave to speak at your business, church, or convention, call 818-735-9503.

Index

Index

Index

Index

Questions, 92–93, 106–107

Reality in organizations, 186–191
  and accountability, 192
  core values aspect, 187–188, 189–191
  critical success factors, 18–19
  performance expectations aspect, 188–191
  vision aspect, 187
Rebellion, 180, 181
Receiving, 71, 154–155
Reconciliation, 94–98
Recruitment, 181–183
Regret vs. execution, 51
Relationships, 133–137, 148, 172–173. *See also*
  People skills
Repentance, 15, 180–181, 191
Repression, 180
Reputation, and partnerships, 172
Resistance to change, 214, 220
Resourcefulness, 165–166
Respect, 117–118, 136–137
Responsibility, accepting, 59
Rest, importance of, 141
Restoration, 180, 181
Risk, fear of, 214, 219–220
Rohn, Jim, 34
Ruth, 200

Samaritans, 119–121
Samson, 72–73
Samuel (prophet), 12, 184–185, 200
Sanballat, 228
Sapphira, 61, 196–197
Satan:
  and Ananias, 196
  asks for Simon, 118–119
  cast out of Heaven, 14, 62
  and distractions, 51
  as father of lies, 81
  possession of Mary of Magdalene, 91
  and pride, 69
  temptation by, 167
Saul (King), 10–11, 12–14, 47, 73, 82
Saul of Tarsus:
  and Barnabas, 200
  conversion to Paul, 48
Scorekeeping, 107–109
Scornfulness, avoiding, 68–69
Second chances, 194–195
Second mile, going, 87–90
Secret giving, 159–160
Secrets, 134

Self-evaluation, 203–204
Self-examination, 98–100, 164
Self-interest, 60–61
Selfishness, 59, 133–134, 205
Selflessness, 124
Self-sufficiency, 153–154
Sermon on the Mount, 188
Service, four C's of, 24, 26
Seven, symbolism of, 91–92
Shadrach, 212
Sheba (Queen), 132
Silas, 210–211
Simon Peter. *See* Peter (Simon Peter) (apostle)
Simon the Zealot (apostle), 27
The Simple Abundance Journal of Gratitude
  (Breathnach), 143
Solomon (King), 61, 131–132, 195, 200
Spiritual balance, 128, 141–146, 148, 150
Spurgeon, Charles, 64, 68, 174
Stanley, Andy, 222
Staying up in down times, 220–226
  clearing out dead weight, 222
  communication, 226
  decision making, 221, 223
  depending on your team, 224–225
  80/20 rule, 223
  emotional control, 225
  empowering your people, 224
  expectations, 222
  expense reduction, 222–223
  financial controls, 224
  leading from the front, 221
  learning from past, 223
  opportunity in crisis, 226
  optimism about future, 225–226
  strategy development, 226
Stephen (disciple), 38, 39
Stereotypes, 184
Straight answers, 92–93
Strategic alliances, 172
Strategic planning, 226
Stress, 128, 135–136, 142
Strong's Exhaustive Concordance of the Bible, 163
Structure, and momentum, 217
Stubbornness, 69
Superiority, feelings of, 67–68
Surrender to God, 74–75
Swearing to your own hurt, 83–85

Talking too much, 105–107
Tarshish, 73
Taxes, 69, 98–99, 170–171

251